Incorporating Montessori Principles into Your Early Years Environments

Incorporating Montessori Principles into Your Early Years Environments will allow readers to understand the developing child in their early years setting and how to adapt a Montessori approach to meet their pupils' needs.

This book shares an insight into Maria Montessori's extensive research, observations, and findings about child development and education, enabling them to transfer these to their own setting. Based on the scientific observation of the child and the stages of development they go through, Montessori pedagogy can be successfully applied in any setting and is well-known for its child-centred, holistic, and individualised approach to education. By addressing its key principles such as respect for the child, prepared environment, and the role of the adult, chapters highlight the overarching vision Montessori's approach had and explore how and why it can still be so meaningful in today's early years classrooms. This book will allow the reader to reflect on the framework they work with and offer examples of adapted practice as well as highlighting the importance of knowing the children, observing their work, and planning suitable resources and activities that will nurture their development.

This is an essential reading for trainee Montessori teachers, trainee educators, early childhood professionals, and childminders, empowering them to enhance learning and development for their pupils, whilst instilling love and respect throughout their interactions with them.

Sarah Cummins is Senior Lecturer in the School of Education, Leeds Trinity University, UK.

"I am pleased to endorse this new contribution to early years libraries on working in early childhood education with Montessori principles. The book expertly explains key concepts from Montessori's approach and their relevance in contemporary early childhood contexts.

This text supports educators to understand the developing child in their early years setting and how to adapt a Montessori approach to meet the child's needs at that time. Starting with the importance of observation and knowing the child, the book offers practical suggestions to help plan appropriate resources and activities.

The author has used their extensive knowledge and experience, bringing together theory and practice to create a text which is rooted in theory and yet is highly practical.

This is a modern, up to date, well-researched and easy-to-follow guide for students, educators, and leaders alike. It reminds us to reconnect with our purpose – to follow the child."

Nathan Archer, *Director, International Montessori Institute, Leeds Beckett University, UK*

"Interest in Montessori pedagogy is increasing as practitioners look for approaches to support young children's holistic development in their early years environments. This is a must have book for education and early years students and practitioners, internationally, who want to develop their knowledge and practice through a Montessori lens. Sarah's intuitive understanding of both the early years child and the Montessori method will enable the reader to understand and reflect through their own cultural lens to create learning environments in which children will flourish and reach their full potential."

Michelle Wisbey, *Senior Lecturer and Course Leader, MA Montessori Education, School of Education and Social Care, Anglia Ruskin University, UK*

Incorporating Montessori Principles into Your Early Years Environments
A Guide to Following the Child

Sarah Cummins

LONDON AND NEW YORK

Designed cover image: © Getty Images

First published 2025
by Routledge
4 Park Square, Milton Park, Abingdon, Oxon OX14 4RN

and by Routledge
605 Third Avenue, New York, NY 10158

Routledge is an imprint of the Taylor & Francis Group, an informa business

© 2025 Sarah Cummins

The right of Sarah Cummins to be identified as author of this work has been asserted in accordance with sections 77 and 78 of the Copyright, Designs and Patents Act 1988.

All rights reserved. No part of this book may be reprinted or reproduced or utilised in any form or by any electronic, mechanical, or other means, now known or hereafter invented, including photocopying and recording, or in any information storage or retrieval system, without permission in writing from the publishers.

Trademark notice: Product or corporate names may be trademarks or registered trademarks, and are used only for identification and explanation without intent to infringe.

British Library Cataloguing-in-Publication Data
A catalogue record for this book is available from the British Library

ISBN: 978-1-032-73965-6 (hbk)
ISBN: 978-1-032-73962-5 (pbk)
ISBN: 978-1-003-46697-0 (ebk)

DOI: 10.4324/9781003466970

Typeset in Galliard
by Apex CoVantage, LLC

Contents

About the Author ix
Acknowledgements x

Introduction 1

1 The Montessori Approach 4

2 Montessori Early Years: The Child, the Adult, and the Prepared Environment 12

3 Observation 22

4 The Planes of Development and the Absorbent Mind 34

5 The Sensitive Periods 44

6 The Prepared Environment 51

7 Play Is Work 63

8 Freedom Within Limits 76

9 Hands-On Learning 83

10 Independence 96

11 Respect 107

12 Language 116

13 Mathematics   129

14 Movement and Wellbeing   140

15 Social and Emotional Development   152

16 Making It Work in Your Environment   158

   Bibliography   *163*
   Index   *165*

About the Author

Sarah Cummins is a senior lecturer in the School of Education at Leeds Trinity University and an education consultant focusing on early years and Montessori practice. Sarah's career spans over 20 years working in settings in North America and the United Kingdom. Sarah is also the chairperson for the Montessori Society UK and sits on the OMEP UK executive committee.

Sarah has a wealth of experience supporting educators, settings, and families in incorporating Montessori principles into their environments.

Sarah is passionate about the importance of the early years and believes that all children deserve an education that embodies love and respect for the child.

Acknowledgements

I have so many people to thank who have encouraged, supported, and inspired me to bring this book to life, but keeping in line with the focus of the book, the child, I would like to thank all the children I have had the honour of being part of their journey in the classroom. You have all inspired me and given me more than I will ever be able to repay. A special thanks to the children at Flitch Green Montessori and Westwood Montessori for sharing your pictures with me for this book. An extra special thanks to my own four children – Eloise, Abigail, Henry, and Michael – who have continued to remind me to trust their journey. It is a privilege to watch you grow, and I am in awe of your zest for life.

My thanks go to Montessori colleagues who work with me to advocate for young children and share Montessori pedagogy with as many people as we can reach. Christine Laubin, Diana Bradley, Michelle Wisbey, Nathan Archer, and Gia Avellini, thank you for your guidance, support, and input in putting this book together. Together, we can inspire the change needed in our early year's education.

In addition, thank you to family, colleagues, and educators who have shared their experiences and stories about Montessori in practice, motivated me throughout this process, and believed in me enough to have inspired me to write this book and share the potential with others. There are too many to name, but you know who you are!

Final thanks go to my parents for fostering a love of learning, offering hands-on experiences, and inspiring me to explore the world, all before I ever knew about Montessori education!

Introduction

> We see the figure of the child who stands before us with his arms held open, beckoning humanity to follow.
> (Montessori, 1992a, Education and Peace)

For over 20 years, I have been working with Montessori in a variety of settings and in different countries. My experiences during this time have helped shape me and inspire me to continue the much-needed work in education to advocate for young children.

Although, without knowing it, my childhood was steeped in Montessori principles. My dad, an engineer, advocated for hands-on experiences for learning and was always creating some resource for me to use when he was reinforcing concepts. I was fortunate enough to have had the opportunities to travel to and live in Asia and America with my family as a child and was empowered my parents to explore all the world had to offer.

My own Montessori education began in Toronto, Canada, and here, everything made sense to me, finally! I felt at home as I learnt the materials and began to understand the writings of Maria Montessori. My training prepared me to be an observer and to trust the child but, at the same time, ready to meet their needs and guide them. It started my journey as an advocate for children's voice and for education to meet their needs.

Continuing my quest to make a difference in the lives of young children, I was a classroom guide, manager, and eventually, a founder and headteacher of a Montessori school. I have always had a sense there was still more to be done, and this has now led me to working with settings around the world incorporating Montessori principles into their settings, embedding Montessori pedagogy in all my work as a senior lecturer to inspire our future educators and policy makers in the world of education, and now writing this book!

An education capable of saving humanity is no small undertaking; it involves the spiritual development of man, the enhancement of his value as an individual, and the preparation of young people to understand the times in which they live.

(Montessori, 1992a, Education and Peace)

There is much work to be done for mankind, and it starts with early years. Around the world, early years educators are not valued or appreciated for their knowledge, expertise, or important positions they hold. Montessori believed that it was the early years education that was the most important – more important than the university years, as it is in early years where the foundation for all future learning is set. Although times have changed since Montessori started her work with children, the fundamental needs of a child have not. This is why the Montessori approach is still relevant today, and there is an urgency to ensure we are not rushing children through childhood and creating problems later in all aspects of their lives.

Montessori herself said she did not create a method of education; she just gave children a chance to live. The Montessori principles can be adapted to any setting, and by educating yourself on the needs of the child, your mind will shift from delivering a curriculum to preparing an environment that meets the needs of the child during their stage of development. Trust the process and follow the child.

How to Use This Book

This book has been written to offer the reader an insight into the principles of Montessori. The focus throughout is the child, but Montessori identified the child was part of a trinity; including the child, the adult, and the prepared environment. Each chapter breaks down the topic in terms of how the content relates to the corresponding part of the trinity.

At some points in the book, you will see I have shared some lesson examples. These were carefully chosen with a focus on the purpose of the activity for the child and the movements within the lesson. These activities are not to suggest the purchase of Montessori materials. The materials are not the necessary component of incorporating the principles into your setting. The lessons are broken down in step-by-step guides, and I would encourage you to practice these at a slow pace. There is no rush!

Within each chapter, I have shared Montessori quotes. These are not only relevant to the topic covered in the chapter but are also there to inspire you to find out more! This book in not the full story; it is the beginning of your journey with Montessori. Even after 20+ years, I am still learning. Reading through Montessori's work in preparation for this book offered me new insights into her pedagogy. I continue to learn from the children I work with and turn back to Montessori for guidance on how to best serve them.

This book does not focus on one government policy. Whatever country you are in, you will be able to address each of the topic's according to the policies and legislations in your country. Remember, our frameworks are guidance.

They do not tell us "how" to teach. We can ensure we meet the requirements of the framework using Montessori principles when we have a greater understanding of the developing child and their needs.

Stand Up for Change!

Change is needed, and by embedding Montessori principles into your settings, you will begin to make that change for the future. You will be empowering our agents of change, the children, to be prepared for their world now and their future world. Education is the peace our world needs and the agent for sustainability.

> Preventing conflict is the work of politics; establishing peace is the work of education.
>
> (Montessori, 1992a, Education and Peace)

1 The Montessori Approach

> **Box 1.1 Chapter Overview**
>
> By the end of this chapter, you will be able to do the following:
>
> - Have a brief understanding of Maria Montessori's life and work.
> - Recognise the influences for Montessori throughout her own development as an educator.
> - Appreciate the barriers and challenges imposed onto Montessori throughout her career.
> - Understand the key principles and key components of the Montessori approach.
> - Understand the relevance of Montessori today and for the future.

The History

Dr. Maria Montessori was born in Italy in 1870 and, throughout her own education journey, broke through barriers which at the time put restraints on women's careers. Standing out as an individual, Montessori had originally intended to study engineering, which at the time was unusual for girls to pursue.

Graduating from school, Montessori was then determined to become a doctor. Her father opposed the idea, as at the time, it was an all-male profession. So much so that Maria Montessori was refused entry to the course. Although a setback, Montessori found another avenue to enter the field of medicine. She enrolled at the University of Rome to study physics, mathematics, and natural sciences. Upon completion of this diploma, she began her studies in medicine and again broke through barriers, as she went on to win several scholarships at medical school.

In 1896, she successfully graduated as one of the first women to obtain a doctor of medicine degree from the University of Rome, with a focus on neurology. That same year, Montessori began to work as a surgical assistant at San Spirito's hospital. Most of her work there was with the poor and their children.

Montessori went beyond the expectations of a physician, tending to her patients with exceptional care, ensuring they were warm and well fed, whilst also treating their illnesses. This perhaps was due to the social expectations or responsibilities as caregivers that many women felt during the nineteenth century.

In 1897, Montessori visited Rome's asylums for children, who at the time were referred to as having "mental disorders." It was this work with those children that went on to change her life. She was consumed with how the children collected crumbs from the floor after they had eaten and began to consider if the children were in fact bored and unstimulated, which was contributing to their conditions.

Later in 1897, as her work with the asylum children was gaining interest, Montessori addressed the National Medical Congress in Turin, advocating for better provision for children with mental and emotional needs. With determination, she expressed her belief that it was the inadequate environments and stimulation that was causing the behaviours of concern. Filled with belief, the following year, Montessori proposed special training for teachers working with children with additional needs.

Keen to understand Edouard Seguin's work, Montessori visited the hospital in Paris where Seguin had further developed Jean Itard's technique of sensorial education in his schools for children with disabilities. Seguin had created practical materials and equipment to support children who were intellectually challenged to develop their sensory perceptions and motor skills.

Montessori went on to become the co-director of a newly founded school for children with a range of disorders, resulting in her transition from medical doctor to educator. Her co-director, Giuseppe Montesano, became a close friend and lover, and in 1898, Maria Montessori gave birth to a son, Mario. At the beginning of the twentieth century, having a child out of wedlock would have been detrimental to Montessori in her personal and professional capacity. Mario was given his mother's name but was given into care of a family near Rome. It is believed that Montessori, struggling with the reality of giving up her own child, turned her attention to meeting the needs of other children. Although Montessori did spend time with Mario as he grew up, it was not until he was older did he find out Maria was his mother.

In 1901, after leaving the school, Montessori continued her own studies at the University of Rome. Through her intense study of the "physiological method" of Edouard Seguin, whom she found great inspiration from, she went on to apply all she had learnt to the education of senses which has become known worldwide as the Montessori approach. She went on to lecture at the Pedagogic School at the University of Rome until 1908.

> The subject of our study is humanity; our purpose is to become teachers. Now, what really makes a teacher is love for the human child; for it is love that transforms the social duty of the educator in the higher consciousness of a mission.
> (Montessori, 1913, Pedagogical Anthropology, quoted in Kramer, 2017)

In 1906, Dr. Montessori was approached to support with an urban renewal project in the San Lorenzo district of Rome, working with children that were most disadvantaged and previously unschooled and whose behaviour was considered a challenge. Montessori relished the opportunity to now bring her work to "typical" children. The first Casa dei Bambini (Children's House) was opened with over 50 children aged between 2 and 6 on January 6, 1907, with Montessori determined to provide a quality environment for these children to learn in.

Whilst the behaviour of the children was a challenge to begin with, they did show interest in activities such as puzzles, cooking, and cleaning. Montessori used her skill of scientific observation to understand the children and what they were doing, and soon, she was observing the children calmer, concentrated, and showing respect to their environment.

Through these insights, Montessori began to further understand the nature of children and only kept the materials that the children engaged in. Montessori recognised that with materials that support the children's interest and needs, within an environment that respects the child's development, children had the power to educate themselves. Within a small number of years, following the progress made by the children, there were five more Casa dei Bambini (Children's House) environments opened. With this brought further intense interest, and visitors would arrive to see the results for themselves. Within a year, part of Switzerland began to transition its kindergarten settings into Casa dei Bambini (Children's House) environments.

Montessori believed these environments were a tool to social change for children and their mothers. She believed mothers should have opportunities to work in the knowledge their children were being cared for and educated in an environment that will support their development. I believe it was Montessori's own experience with her son that led to her being a strong advocate for women in this way. In 1909, she not only gave her first teacher training course on her method, but she also published her first book, The Montessori method, becoming influential in the world of education and remains so today. The Montessori approach to education has become a widely acclaimed philosophy that emphasises the natural development of a child through self-directed learning, hands-on activities, and a carefully prepared environment.

Following much worldwide travel, with her son, Mario, speaking about her approach and children's development and offering training of teachers, she went on to receive three Nobel Peace Prize nominations. In 1952, Maria Montessori, with Mario by her side, died in the Netherlands. Mario went on to continue her life's work after her death.

> I did not invent a method of education; I simply gave little children a chance to live.
>
> (Montessori [1914], 1970, Maria Montessori:
> A Centenary Anthology 1870–1970)

Philosophical Foundations

At the heart of the Montessori method lies a profound respect for the child's individuality and intrinsic desire to learn. Dr. Montessori truly believed that every child is born with an inner drive for self-construction and that the role of education is to support and guide rather than impose external agendas. "Following the child" is at the core of this philosophical approach, where specially trained educators observe and respond to the individual, unique needs, and interests of the child, supporting them to progress at their own pace and offering opportunities for them to explore subjects that ignite their curiosity.

Early childhood is a critical period of rapid growth and development, laying the foundation for a child's whole life learning and wellbeing. Montessori focuses on honouring the natural curiosity, independence, and developmental needs and stages of the young child.

The Montessori philosophy considers children as active participants in their own learning, capable of great achievements, constructing their own understanding of the world around them through exploration and discovery.

> Children learn naturally through activity and their characters develop through freedom.
>
> (Montessori, 2007b, Maria Montessori Speaks to Parents)

Montessori supports the full development of the human being, and its approach offers a concept of education as an "aid to life." Montessori inspires children towards a lifelong love of learning by following their own natural development journey.

Montessori education is child-led and self-paced learning in a secure, nurturing environment that is guided by caring and knowledgeable adults. Individual children will take the time they need to explore their interests and curiosity, at their own pace, to fully understand each concept. Through the multi-sensory approach, children are also afforded opportunities for independence, accountability, and citizenship.

Key Principles of the Montessori Method

The philosophy created by Dr. Montessori is not a theory that was concocted and then applied to children but is based upon many years of observation of children. Montessori considered her philosophy as a complete social movement that has universal application. This means that Dr. Montessori believed that no matter what country, religion, or background a child is from, their development is approximately the same.

Aside from the universal application, there are several other basic principles that guide her philosophy. Whilst these principles will be covered in more detail throughout later chapters, it is important to begin with a basic understanding:

- Children learn by doing – they need to touch, to try, and to advance by doing.
- Children love work – they have a different motivation for work than adults do and will prefer it to "playing." Note: A child's work is their play.
- Children should be offered maximum spontaneity – when they show an interest in something, they should be allowed to pursue it.
- There should be a profound respect for the child – we should see all children in early years as basically benevolent.
- Rewards and punishments should not be used – both are coercions and do not assist the child towards self-discipline, which should be the goal.
- Each child should be dealt with as an individual in their educational process – a balance of adult-led, individually chosen and group activities support the child to build autonomy at their own pace.
- Children learn best from each other, rather than from the adult.
- Children work at their own individual pace and should not be rushed or slowed by the adult.
- There should be no competitiveness in the environment. Cohesiveness and collaboration support social development.
- Development of the whole personality should always be considered – the mind, the body, and the spirit are inextricably connected in children.

1. **Prepared Environment:** Montessori environments are carefully considered and designed to meet the needs of the developing child. The furniture, materials, and space invite movement and exploration. The environment is carefully curated to promote independence, order (understanding of the world, clear, logical, and sequential thinking), and a sense of security and belonging, providing the child with the freedom to engage in purposeful activities. This also applies to the preparation of the adult.
2. **Hands-On Learning:** Montessori highlighted the relationship between the child's hand and brain and observed that children learn by doing. Activities are specifically designed to appeal to a young child's senses and designed to give the child a concrete, hands-on learning experience. Children are developing life skills whilst exploring with their senses.
3. **The Planes of Development:** Montessori highlighted that all children exhibit characteristics and needs in four distinct stages that she termed "planes of development." Understanding and recognising these planes of development aid us in our quest to support the child's development and learning.
4. **Absorbent Mind:** Children constantly learn from their world through exploration. Montessori determined that the first six years of the child's life are the most crucial in a child's development and that children had the ability to absorb all their environment has to offer.
5. **Sensitive Periods:** Montessori observed that children go through specific stages in their development when they are most capable of learning

particular skills. These sensitive periods are windows of opportunity when the child is particularly receptive to acquiring these human attributes.

6. **Child at the Centre of the Approach:** In Montessori, the adults serve as guides and facilitators who observe, support, and promote the child's learning experiences. Children are encouraged to follow their own interests and develop their agency in a supportive environment. Children are supported in choosing activities independently, taking ownership over their learning. Having the child at the centre of the approach promotes intrinsic motivation and a deep love of learning, as children are afforded the opportunity to explore topics and materials at their own pace and in their own way.
7. **Mixed-Age Grouping:** Montessori classrooms feature mixed-age groupings, typically spanning three-year age ranges, aligning with the planes of development. Mixed-age grouping allow for our younger children to learn from and be motivated by older peers, whilst our older children develop leadership skills and empathy through mentoring younger peers. Mixed-age groupings also promote collaboration, socialisation, and a sense of belonging, reflecting the natural diversity of the real world and supporting a child's social and emotional development.
8. **Respect for the Whole Child:** Montessori recognised academic achievement is enhanced because Montessori education embraces holistic development of the child. Montessori understood that all aspects of learning and development were integrated. All aspects of the Montessori curriculum incorporate opportunities for movement, outdoor learning and play, creative expression, conflict resolution, and social learning, nurturing a child's wellbeing.
9. **Freedom within Limits:** Montessori believed that children were capable of learning and doing for themselves and should be empowered to discover their capabilities, interests, and self at their own pace within an environment that has been prepared to the needs of the child. The limits come within the environment and are considered the expectations of the environment for all to be a community working together.
10. **The Role of the Adult:** In the Montessori world, the teacher is often referred to as the guide rather than the teacher, and this reflects how Montessori believed that adults are there to facilitate and guide the child to their own self-discovery as a human.
11. **Observation:** Montessori viewed observation as the key to understanding the child to be able to meet their needs. Observation is a skill to be developed to avoid judgment and assumption or opinion when understanding the needs of the child.

Montessori Everyday – A Way of Life

Montessori principles can be applied to everyday life, not just in a Montessori educational setting. Montessori can be carried into every educational setting serving children, homes, childcare provisions, hospitals, community homes, and in every interaction with children.

> If education is always to be conceived a mere transmission of knowledge, there is little to be hoped from it in the bettering of (our) future. For what is the use of transmitting knowledge if the individual's total development lags behind?. The Child is endowed with unknown powers, which can guide us to a radiant future. If what we really want is a new world, then education must take as its aim the development of these hidden possibilities.
> (Montessori, 1949, The Absorbent Mind)

Current Landscape of Montessori Education

In the ever-changing landscape of education worldwide, many ask if Montessori is still relevant, and the short answer is "yes"! Montessori recognised the need for change all those years ago, but sadly, education has not moved on as much as it could or needs to be. Today, there have been great advances, such as technology, but the development of the child has not changed.

> Times have changed, and science has made great progress, and so has our work; but our principles have only been confirmed, and along with them our conviction that mankind can hope for a solution to its problems, among which the most urgent are those of peace and unity, only by turning its attention and energies to the discovery of the child and to the development of the great potentialities of the human personality in the course of its formation.
> (Montessori, 1972b, The Discovery of the Child)

Montessori wanted her approach to working with children to be available to everyone, and this is why her name is not protected. This means any setting can call themselves Montessori, and it is because of this that greater sharing of the Montessori approach is needed. Unfortunately, and not by design, there are more private Montessori schools around the world than public, making it a challenge for many families to attend. Persuading policy makers to fund Montessori education, offering families an alternative, is the biggest challenged faced. Montessori never intended her approach to be for the select few that could afford it.

In fact, many early years settings would consider themselves unable to afford the specialised Montessori materials, but generally, the materials cost no more than some of the other less effective toys in some settings. This misconception, that Montessori lies in the materials, results in some settings purchasing Montessori materials that are inappropriate for the age group they serve and employing no trained staff to implement the ethos. Montessori herself recognised her approach was not about the materials; it was always about following the child.

Montessori for Sustainability

The focus of Montessori education remains around the child's natural development and growth. This development is not bound by socio-economic status or culture. No technology or scientific advancement can adjust the progress of human development. Montessori firmly believed that the role of education is to empower the children as future stewards of the world we live in.

When we consider sustainability in early childhood, we are referring to the approach to education and childcare that emphasises fostering a sense of collaboration, mutual respect, responsibility, awareness and care for the environment, society, and future generations. Montessori recognised the importance of community in the development of the whole child and the impact this will have on future lives.

By incorporating Montessori principles into your practice, homes, and general lives, you can help young children develop a sense of belonging, empathy, and responsibility within their local community and the broader global context. Cultivating well-rounded individuals who appreciate the interconnectedness of all people and the importance of contributing positively to the world around them can only bring more goodness into our lives now and for future generations to come!

The Montessori approach has a strong emphasis on fostering children's voice, rights, and empowerment by recognising their individual capabilities and respecting their autonomy. They are the change agents we need to create a world that is sustainable.

Summary

Following on from her early career in medicine, Montessori went on to develop an education based on her findings from her observations of children and addressed their needs during different developmental stages. Montessori recognised the importance of the early years and the role adults play in protecting the child and providing them with optimal learning opportunities. Montessori developed her approach to education emphasising respect for the child, individualised learning, and the importance of the prepared environment to support the holistic development of the child.

Montessori believed that children all over the world had the same fundamental needs and wanted all children to have access to her method. Following the child, adapting to their evolving needs and interests as they progress through different developmental stages, she believed the child was the answer to peace and harmony in the world, and they should be respected for all they are capable of. Montessori education today is not accessible to all children, and now more than ever, we need to change that. Montessori education empowers the child and prepares them to develop as capable, independent, curious, and confident global citizens and agents of change.

2 Montessori Early Years
The Child, the Adult, and the Prepared Environment

Box 2.1 Chapter Overview

By the end of this chapter, you will be able to do the following:

- Understand the connections between the child, the adult, and the prepared environment.
- Understand your role as the adult in observation and preparation of the environment.
- Explore how these connections foster optimal learning experiences and support natural development in young children.

Introduction

Considering the vast landscape of early childhood, the Montessori approach emerges as a masterpiece and a beacon of holistic development, emphasising the pivotal roles played by the child, the adult, and the prepared environment. Montessori believed that the child's innate potential was nurtured through a harmonious interplay between the child's natural curiosity and desire to learn, the supportive guidance of the adult, and the meticulously curated prepared environment. Dr. Montessori recognised the child's innate capacity for self-directed exploration and growth, thus placing the child at the centre of her approach.

At the heart of the Montessori method lies a profound respect for the child's individuality and intrinsic desire to learn. Dr. Montessori truly believed that every child is born with an inner drive for self-construction and that the role of education is to support and guide rather than impose external agendas. "Following the child" is at the core of this philosophical approach, where educators observe and respond to the individual, unique needs, and interests of the child, supporting them to progress at their own pace and offering opportunities for them to explore subjects that ignite their curiosity.

DOI: 10.4324/9781003466970-3

Now the adult himself is part of the child's environment; the adult must adjust himself to the child's needs if he is not to be a hindrance to him and if he is not to substitute himself for the child in the activities essential to growth and development.
>
> (Montessori, 1977, The Secret of Childhood)

Early childhood is a critical period of rapid growth and development, laying the foundation for a child's future learning and wellbeing. Montessori focuses on honouring the natural curiosity, independence, and developmental needs and stages of the young child. The Montessori philosophy considers children as active participants in their own learning, capable of remarkable things, constructing their own understanding of the world around them through exploration and discovery.

> Children learn naturally through activity and their characters develop through freedom.
>
> (Montessori, 2007, Maria Montessori Speaks to Parents)

Montessori supports the full development of the human being, and its approach offers a concept of education as an "aid to life." Montessori inspires children towards a lifelong love of learning by following their own natural development journey.

Montessori education is child-led and self-paced learning in a secure, nurturing environment that is guided by caring and knowledgeable adults. Individual children will take the time they need to explore their interests and curiosity, at their own pace, to fully understand each concept. Through the multi-sensory approach, children are also afforded opportunities for independence, accountability, and citizenship.

As mentioned, respect is at the heart of the Montessori philosophy, and this means we also recognise the profound importance of the child at the centre of all we do as adults, and it is our role to understand and value the child's needs and offer opportunities for exploration and growth within an environment that is prepared to meet the child's needs.

It is important to note here that when we say "the child," we are referring to the individual child. No two children are the same nor do they develop at the same pace. It is through observation and understanding the development of children that enables the adult to support the needs of the child. Montessori emphasised the importance of the relationship between the child, the adult, and the prepared environment. This relationship should grow and evolve, based on the observation of children and identification of their needs.

The Child

Montessori valued each child as an individual and championed for their individuality to be celebrated. She modelled how adults should respect and honour the child's uniqueness, and rather than trying to fit the child into the expectations of the adult, the adult should meet the child where they are at and provide opportunities for them to grow and develop.

Montessori believed that children developed in stages (see Chapter 4), and each unique stage has its own characteristics. Each stage sees physical, cognitive, emotional, and spiritual changes for the child. The four stages that Montessori referred to are as follows:

Infancy/early childhood: birth to 6 (birth to 3 – unconscious absorbent mind; 3 to 6 – conscious absorbent mind)
Childhood: 6 to 12 (3 to 6 and 6 to 12)
Adolescence: 12 to 18
Maturity: 18 to 24

For this book, the focus will be the early childhood stage. This is a very special stage where vast growth occurs as the child absorbs naturally, without effort, all that is around them.

> There is in the child a special kind of sensitivity which leads him to absorb everything about him and it is this work of observing and absorbing that alone enables him to adapt himself to life. He does it in virtue of an unconscious power that exists in childhood. . . . The first period of the child's life is one of adaptation.
> (Montessori, 1964, The Absorbent Mind)

Characteristics of this Stage

- Development of the senses
- Development of language
- Formation of basic habits and skills

Think of the young child as the discoverer of life. They are thirsty to interact with the environment and absorb all the information about the world. They are keen explorers as they figure out their place in their world. During the first three years, all learning occurs outside the child's conscious mind. They learn by exploring their senses. Think about the infant finding their hands and then wanting to taste everything. The child then starts to consciously seek out experiences and information. They start to develop a strong sense of individuality and a determination to do things for themselves. We see this in children not wanting our help ("let me do it") or the child that demonstrates their will with strength and determination! This should be embraced rather than shadowed.

The Adult

> Adults must defend children. We Adults must see the real humanity in children, the humanity which will take our place one day, if we are to have social progress. Social progress means that the next generation is better than the one before.
> (Montessori, 1946, The London Lectures)

In the Montessori world, you will hear the adult being referred to as "the guide" or "directress/director" rather than the teacher. The role of the adult is seen as the facilitator in supporting the child's individual needs and empowering the child's unique individuality. Montessori emphasised that the role and responsibilities of the educator is not that of a disseminator of information but one who creates the opportunities and conditions conducive for learning. This is not about a relationship of knowledge exchange; it is the construction of knowledge. We must start to shift our view that education is something that is done to the child and recognise that it comes from the child. Observe the child, and they will show you what they need.

> An ordinary teacher cannot be transformed into a Montessori teacher, but must be created anew, having rid herself of pedagogical prejudices.
> (Montessori, 1989c, Education for a New World)

There is no greater task than guiding new generations on their journey. The adult must be prepared to see the child through an objective lens and remove judgment or assumption. To do this, the adult must reflect on their own mindset to be fully committed to guiding the child. In preparation of self, the adult must positively develop the following:

- Knowledge of the child
- Knowledge of the subjects being taught
- Knowledge of the resources used
- Knowledge of the community being served
- Humility and modesty
- Humour
- Love and respect
- Responsibility
- A love of their work

The adult should become the following:

- An observer of the child
- An integral part of the child's environment
- The introductory provider of the appropriate materials/activities for the child
- A keeper of the environment
- A provider of boundaries that align with the child's development

The adult, as a guide for the child, must model the protection of the environment. They must care for the environment to maintain beauty and order. The adult will know that this order of the environment will aid in the development of focus and concentration for the child, and the beauty of the environment will not only support this but will also embed a sense of belonging and pride within the child.

The adult will recognise the moments when a child is absorbed in their work or engrossed in a topic. This is the moment the adult will know how best to guide the child next. The adult must never interrupt the child's concentration, not even to praise him. This concentrated moment will be protected and observed, as it gives us an insight into the child's needs and interests. The goal of the observation should be to help the child.

In Montessori, when an adult shows a child how to use a new piece of material/resource, it is called "presenting." I mention this here because it is important for us to remember that children are not born just knowing how to use what we are offering them. They do need to be showed, and these "presentations" need to be carefully planned, giving enough time to the presentation and ensuring the child is ready for this work.

Presentations can be done one to one, small groups, or whole groups, depending on the activity and depending on the needs of the child. The adult needs to be confident of their own abilities and knowledge prior to presenting to the child, and we remember that the presentation goal is to enable the child to work independently. The presentation done by the adult will show the child accurate use of the activity/material with slow and purposeful movements. It is the material that will teach the child, not the adult.

Everything presented must be done in slow, purposeful, simple steps for the child. The child watches and absorbs the movements of the adult with the material, and each movement is shared in a way the child can be successful on their own. During these presentations, the child watches only. They do not touch the material or question the work of the adult. At the end of the presentation, the child is invited to repeat, and typically, the adult will leave the child but be close by, observing.

> She observes in order to recognise the child who has attained the power to concentrate and to admire the glorious rebirth of his spirit.
> (Montessori, 1949, The Absorbent Mind)

The Prepared Environment

Montessori believed that the child's environment should facilitate and maximise independence, learning, and exploration.

> Children acquire knowledge through experience in the environment.
> (Montessori, 1946, The London Lectures)

Referring to the child's environment as the prepared environment emphasises the consideration, time, structure, and order within the space, where everything has a purpose and everything has a place, all within access of the small child. The prepared environment should activate curiosity and a love of learning.

The environment is carefully prepared by the knowledgeable adult who is aware of the needs and interests of the children to create optimal learning experiences. The space itself is neutral, open plan, with a sense of order and beauty. This idea of neutrality is often met with friction, but this is to bring a sense of calm to the child's mind to enable them to focus on their interests. Unnecessary overstimulation distracts the child.

Features of a Prepared Environment

- Structure and order
- Clearly defined areas within the environment (curriculum areas)
- Materials/activities displayed in a progressive order
- Left-to-right orientation
- Freedom of movement
- Freedom of choice
- Freedom within limits
- Focus of independence
- Social environment

Order

The prepared environment offers a calm and structured learning space where children feel secure and know what to expect. This can be adapted to all settings, including home. There should be defined areas for curriculum focus/topics and enough space for work to be done at a table or on the floor.

Child-Sized

Have you ever noticed how frustrating it can be for a child in an adult-sized world? They are desperate to be independent and do it themselves but are being held back. The prepared environment should have child-sized furniture, accessible low and open shelves, and materials/activities that easily fit into the child's hand.

Reality

Where possible, the use of real-life objects provides the children with real-life learning experiences that not only build their relationship with the world around them but also their confidence for real-life situations.

Beauty

Offer beauty to the child: a clean, orderly, and neutral environment, with mostly natural materials, all displayed with care and consideration for the child. Any displays on the wall should be neatly displayed at the child's level in a dedicated space.

Freedom and Choice

The prepared environment should offer freedom of movement, freedom of time, and freedom of choice. Children should be guided to follow their own interests without time restrictions and also choose where they do their work (floor/table). Children should be offered choice when options are available.

Left-to-Right Progression

The materials on the shelves should be displayed from left to right in a progressive order, increasing in difficulty and challenge as the child moves on. This structure is an indirect preparation to future learning (reading and writing).

Freedom Within Limits

Children have the freedom to follow their own interest, move freely within their environment, and have the freedom to choose their learning, if the "ground rules" of their environment is being respected.

Independence

The prepared environment should be prepared to enable and facilitate children to develop their independence. Children are afforded the opportunities to think for themselves and to do for themselves as much as possible and safe to do so.

Social Environment

The prepared environment enables natural social interaction to occur which facilitates the emotional development of the child. Children learn how to be part of a community and develop a sense of compassion and empathy.

The prepared environments are for the child prepared by the adults. They are carefully organised to support the developing needs of the child and promote active engagement in learning. It is important to note here that prepared environments can be adapted to any culture or setting.

Box 2.2 Reflection Practice Exercise

Look around the environment you are providing for the child/ren.

- Is it inviting? Is it engaging?
- Are there enough materials on the shelves to meet the needs of the child?
- Is there order and structure?
- Is it accessible for the child?

Now get down to the child's level and explore the environment. Move around at this level or take a picture of the different areas from the child's level, and consider the earlier questions again and then consider the following:

- Are there barriers to movement in the environment?
- Is there too much open space (a runway)?
- Are the shelves clean and tidy?
- Are the activities inviting?

The Relationship Between the Child, the Adult, and the Prepared Environment

Respect (see Chapter 11).

The relationship in this trinity is built on respect.

In all aspects of Montessori's principles, respect is interwoven and at the core of her pedagogy. It is evident from the care and consideration that is put into preparing environments that serve the needs of the developing child, the way children are trusted and encouraged to be active participants in their own learning.

The adult is there to guide and facilitate, but to do that, they observe the child; they FOLLOW THE CHILD.

> When a child is given a little leeway, he will at once shout, "I want to do it!" But in our schools, which have an environment adapted to children's needs, they say, "Help me to do it alone."
> (Montessori, 1972a, The Secret of Childhood)

The "follow the child" statement is often heard in Montessori settings, but it is applicable to every environment in a child's life, school, home, or elsewhere. To follow the child is to believe the child has the capabilities to drive their own learning, and our role it to prepare the environment and then step aside.

Traditional education is based on the opposite, where there is a curriculum the teacher must adhere to. The teacher makes the curriculum interesting and engaging, but the child follows the teacher. Montessori observed the inner drive children had to learn. Montessori saw that children start to develop their identity and a passion for all they do and believed it was the role of the adult to prepare the child's environments to meet their needs and facilitate this inner drive.

Box 2.3 Reflective Task

Reflective practice is essential for adults working with children to continually evaluate and improve the relationship with the children. Here are some reflective tasks you can engage in to consider your relationship with children.

1. Self-awareness: Reflect on your own belief, attitudes, and biases about children. Consider how these factors influence your work with them. Ask yourself the following:

   - What are my personal beliefs about children's capabilities and development?
   - How do my past experiences with children shape my interactions with them?
   - Am I aware of any biases or stereotypes that may affect how I perceive and interact with children?

2. Observe and Reflect: Regularly observe your interactions with children and reflect on them afterwards. Consider the following:

   - How do I communicate with children? Am I attentive and responsive to their needs and interests?
   - Am I providing opportunities for children to express themselves and make choices?
   - How are the children responding to my actions and words? Are there any patterns in their behaviour towards my actions or words?

3. Seek Feedback: Actively seek feedback from colleagues, parents, and of course, the children themselves about your interactions. Ask for specific examples or instances where your interactions were particularly effective or could have been improved. Consider the following:

   - What feedback am I receiving about my interactions with children?
   - Are there areas where I could enhance my communication or relationship-building skills?
   - Self-assess: Would I benefit from support to develop my relationships with the children (coaching)?

Montessori Early Years 21

Figure 2.1 The Child, the Adult, and the Prepared Environment

Summary

The child, the adult, and the prepared environment are a trinity. When the knowledgeable adult prepares a favourable environment, the child become an independent and active learner. If you can combine the right blend of the adult who cares and is passionate and aware of the child's developmental needs with an environment that is carefully curated to meet those needs, you will see the emergence of an independent, capable, active child who is fully engaged in their own learning journey.

This combination takes time, awareness, reflection, and commitment, but ultimately, the child will guide the adult to their needs.

3 Observation

> **Box 3.1 Chapter Overview**
>
> By the end of this chapter, you will be able to do the following:
>
> - Understand what observation is and what it isn't!
> - Examine how observations can take place for different settings.
> - Discuss the different types of observations.
> - Consider the benefits to observation.

Introduction

Montessori believed that observation was the key tool for not only understanding the child but also for creating an environment that meets their needs and supports their development. She believed that approaching observation as a scientific process is necessary to fully understand the child. As an adult, it is often assumed that we know what is best for the child, but through observation, we will gain a greater depth of understanding to help them grow and progress. The child will show us what we need to know.

> Scientific observation then has established that education is not what the teacher gives; education is a natural process spontaneously carried out by the human individual and is acquired not by listening to words but by experiences upon the environment.
>
> (Montessori, 1963, Education for a New World)

To begin with, it is important to remind ourselves that when we observe inanimate objects, we are dealing with things that have no spirit. They do not care what we say about them, and what we do say will not affect their future. When we are dealing with children, we must remember that what we say and what we do will always influence them. We must, therefore, be more cautious about what we say and do.

There is much more to the art of observing than watching and recording information the child has done. Observation is the process of objectively monitoring children to understand what they need. We need to be knowledgeable about child development to effectively observe to be able to act upon what we have observed. Approaching observation like a scientist requires some self-awareness to proceed without judgment, and observing without interference can support the child to gain a sense of independence and competence. Observe as if you have never met this child and know nothing about them! By removing the prior knowledge you have of the child, this allows you to see the child in that moment with fresh eyes.

Observing children helps adults identify the developmental stages (see Chapters 4 and 5) the child is in and helps us recognise the value of the natural development of the child. It allows us to track the progress of a child without interference or hinderance to their development. An effective observer accepts the child where they are at and follows their direction. If the observer applies judgment, Montessori believed they would not be able to assess the skills of the child.

> Even when helping and serving the children, she (the teacher) must not cease to observe them because the birth of concentration in a child is as delicate a phenomenon as the bursting of a bud into bloom.
> (Montessori, 1967, The Absorbent Mind)

Observation has many benefits to both the child and the adults. Adults can use observation to help them prepare their environment to meet the needs of the children. According to Montessori, the prepared environment is vital for the children to learn.

Observation and the Child

For the child, observation enables them to foster their sense of independence and competence. During observation, the adult is showing trust to the child and persuading them to explore on their own and follow their own direction. The child can learn at their own pace during this time, and this freedom gives them a sense of competence which fuels their desire for independence. Montessori highlighted the importance of learning to follow the child, and this can be a challenge for many adults. To follow the child means you allow them to captain their environment. You do not interrupt them or correct them. Instead, you allow them to show you the world from their perspective.

Montessori recognised the value in observation as a tool to better understand the child. It is like getting to look through the lens of their abilities, interests, and personal characteristics. It is the gift that keeps on giving the more you observe! By following the child through observation, they are sharing their needs with you, and you will be able to determine what activities will best serve their need. You use this knowledge to form part of your planning.

The child's sensitive periods (see Chapter 5) will become clearer through observation, again leading the way for you to offer more opportunities for that sensitive period.

Necessary for successful observation is letting the child lead. Let the child show you what you need to know about them. They are communicating with you through their movements, decisions, actions, and choices, and from this, you will be more inclined to know what the child enjoys, what they avoid, how they interact with their peers, how they manage and solve problems or challenges that arise, and much more.

Whilst we recognise the benefits of observation of the child, we need to acknowledge the importance and value of the child's own observation of us or their peers. Children, from the time they are born, are skilled observers. Think about the newborn baby; they simply learn by being and observing. They do not need to be taught to talk or walk; they do so by simply observing.

It is so valuable for children to observe the adults in their lives as well as their peers. Have you ever found yourself commenting about a child who is "doing nothing" or "avoiding doing work for themselves"? Perhaps they are working hard, observing. So much learning is occurring for the child.

Observation and the Adult

> Often inexperienced teachers place great importance on teaching and believe they have done everything necessary when they have demonstrated the use of the materials in a meaningful way. In reality, they are far from the truth because the job of the teacher is rather more important than that. To her falls the task of guiding the development of the child's spirit, and therefore her observations of the child are not to be limited solely to understanding him. All her observations must emerge at the end – and this is their only justification – in her ability to help the child.
>
> (Montessori, 1989a, The Child in the Family)

As the adult in the setting, our own cultural exposure can limit our knowledge of what we are seeing (i.e., a "naughty" child). We certainly don't know everything the child is exposed to. We affect the observation just by being there, so we must ensure we are not being intrusive when we do observe. It is also necessary to be mindful of what we assume by association (e.g., the child with water on their clothes, next to the overflowing water in the sink, may not be the one who left the tap running).

Our early years children are changing at an immense rate on a daily, weekly, and yearly basis that we should always look with a fresh set of eyes. When observing, we focus on the facts of what we see. We speak in terms of what we see and not what you don't see (e.g., "the child doesn't do any work" – What are they doing?).

The role of the teacher is to set up an environment to promote and encourage individualised learning. Observation can be used to determine what the children want to learn and what their skill capabilities are. The prepared environment will then be set up to help the child succeed. When you follow the child, you begin to gain an understanding of the inner work of their mind. You learn to understand their motives and their behaviours and can empathise. Learning from and following the child means you are meeting them where they are and not where you expect them to be.

> Follow the child, they will show you what they need to do, what they need to develop in themselves, and what area they need to be challenged in. The aim of the children who persevere in their work with an object is certainly not to "learn"; they are drawn to it by the needs of their inner life, which must be recognised and developed by its means.
> (Montessori, 1965a, Spontaneous Activity in Education)

With all that said, it is important to understand that following the child does not mean they can do what they like without consequences. It is, however, about following the pattern of the child. Get to know their rhythm. We use the observation to know if the child needs more time or needs to be moved on. Observe the child with curiosity – curious about their choices and their behaviours.

I cannot just say "observe the child," and by magic, all the benefits of observation become obvious! It takes time, skill, and repetition. Montessori stressed the importance of giving the observer the power and means for observation, and these are produced through the education of the senses.

Skills required to observe:

1. Stillness
2. Introspection
3. Silence
4. Flexibility
5. Knowledge

Observation is a skill that requires time and practice to perfect!

> Even when helping and serving the children, she (the teacher) must not cease to observe them, because the birth of concentration in a child is as delicate a phenomenon as the bursting of a bud into bloom.
> (Montessori, 1949, The Absorbent Mind)

Observation and the Prepared Environment

Observations of the prepared environment are essential to ensure the environment is still meeting the needs of the children. These observations will enable reflection, such as the following:

- Does this environment encourage and allow independence?
- Are the children inspired by the activities on offer? Are they being challenged?

- Does the environment flow in beauty and order?
- Is the environment creating any barriers for the child/ren?
- Does the environment encourage social and emotional development?
- Do the children have freedom of movement?

Observations helps us be aware of the physical and psychological aspects of the prepared environment, ensuring we are always focused on the child's needs and taking guidance from what we observe. Our observations are why we adjust or change our prepared environments. They aid us in planning and preparation of the environment as well as the activities we offer the child. To prepare the environment as a community where children are encouraged to be independent, have a sense of responsibility, free to express themselves, and be active agents of change and participants in their own learning, observation is key.

Observation should become a normal part of the environment. Be it the guides or visitors that are observing, the children become accustomed to this practice that it does not hinder their concentration or focus. When you do have visitors observe in your setting, ensure to share your knowledge on how to observe with them (see figure 3.2 later) so they, too, can get the most out of their observation.

Types of Observations

Montessori spoke about three different types of observation:

1. The direct observation of the self (self-observation – awareness of own feelings, biases, thoughts, or reactions)
2. The direct observation of the child (purposeful and attentive observation of the child) (formal)
3. The indirect observation (observation whilst carrying out other tasks, e.g., when working with a child) (informal)

Each of these observations are beneficial and most effective in combination of all three.

How to Observe in Practice

Montessori was a scientist and applied her skills as a scientific observer to her work with children. It is necessary to remember this when we start to observe: we must continue to observe as if we are scientists and leave judgment and opinion aside. We are observing the facts.

Before we begin to observe the child, we must begin with self-observation. To objectively observe a child, we require our minds to be free of distractions and know why we are observing, what our motives are for the observation, and if we can give the time required to objectively observe. It is only then we are ready to observe the child. This self-observation will highlight if we are in fact a contributor of negativity to a situation or perhaps an interference. It will enable us to reflect on our responses to situations.

Getting started with observation can be a challenge. The how to observe, the when to observe, and the what to observe are the most common questions for those wishing to get started with making observation work for them, the child, and their setting. Observation can become your secret weapon to understanding the child and preparing their environment to meet their needs. A few simple starting points are as follows:

1. Calm Environment – Find a place to observe that is comfortable but free from distraction for you to enable you to focus on the child/ren. Do not impose yourself onto the child or make it uncomfortably obvious you are observing them! Let the child do what they are doing and keep judgment away.
2. Be Patient – Stay in your observation spot, fully focused on the child and their movement, activities, and interactions. Let them go at their pace and hold back the urge to intervene.
3. Record Observations – Whilst not all observations need to be formally recorded, it is good practice to write down all the child is doing. You don't need to go into great depth with your descriptions; just jot down notes or time frames of work the child is doing. You can use these recording to track progress, monitor habits, and look for guidance on any necessary adjustments. If you are going to take a picture of a child working during your observation, be sure that task is not disturbing their work.

In short, start now but start with short bursts of formal observation, perhaps 10 to 15 minutes. Focus on one child, sit comfortably, and watch their movements, interactions, and choices, and make note of the facts, not why you think they have chosen something, just what they have chosen. It is good practice to make note of the time with every observation you make. Write down your observations of the following:

- Physical development – Did the child use gross motor skills? If so, what were they? Did the child use fine motor skills? If so, what were they? What physical movements did the child make?
- Language development – Did you observe the child listening, speaking, reading, writing? What language skills did the child use? If so, what were they?
- Cognitive development – What did you observe the child working on? Have they mastered this activity? What are they interested in? Are they repeating work?

- Social development – How is the child interacting with others?
- Emotional development – Did you observe a shift in emotions for the child during your observation? If so, why? Did they laugh, become angry, cry, or frustrated? Did they express these emotions with language or actions?

Box 3.2 Reflective Practice

Example 1: Consider the Following Statements

1. Michael has not engaged in a lot of work this morning. He worked with caring for plants and clay. Michael loves caring for plants. Michael enjoys wiping the leaves and feeding water to the leaves.
2. Between 9.15 and 9.40, Michael took care of plants from the environment. At 9.40, Michael started to paint plants using two colours for the leaves and a different colour for the pots. Michael sits next to the large plant and refers to it whilst creating his clay plants.

Statement 1 is full of judgment and assumption. How do you know Michael loves caring for plants or enjoys wiping the leaves? Was Michael engaged in the work he was doing?

Statement 2 offers a non-judgmental observation that is stating a fact. For a period, Michael took care of plants and used clay. Michael created a clay plant after caring for the real plants.

To move forward with this observation, observe Michael again at a different time or another day to observe his choices of activity. Is it the art activities that has Michael's interest? Is it plants Michael is interested in? Is it linked to other work (science, botany work, flower arranging, etc.) he is doing in the environment? Does he choose this activity independently or guided towards this work?

Moving away from the curriculum, what else was possibly observed?

- Motor development?
- Focus and concentration?
- Sequencing?
- Perseverance?
- Problem solving?
- Critical thinking?

To truly get to know more about Michael, observe again. Observe often. Follow the child.

Figure 3.1 Observing Michael Care for a Plant

Example 2: Consider the Following

Observation notes 1: Henry spat out his peas at lunch because he didn't like them.
Observation notes 2: Henry spat out his peas during lunch, scrunched his face, and said, "No."

Whilst it would be easy to assume that Henry does not like peas, it could be the texture or the temperature that he didn't like. Reflect on what language you are using during observations and how that might be influencing how you respond to the child.

How to Use Your Observations

> She [the teacher] observes in order to recognise the child who has attained the power to concentrate and to admire the glorious rebirth of his spirit.
> (Montessori, 1949, The Absorbent Mind)

Sometimes an observation is just that and nothing more. There is nothing for you to do with the observation. You can note it as a part of the child's progress tracker or for further consideration, but not all observations are formal. They are snapshots of the child's development.

Observations can, however, become the tool by which the adult can consider if the environment is working for the child, if the child needs additional presentations/guidance with a concept or skill, if a child or group of children lose concentration at a particular time of the day, if there is a pattern in the child emerging, etc. They can be used to monitor behaviour to see if there is false fatigue occurring or if the child is having challenges with a peer or perhaps transition.

With an open mind, read over your observation notes, reflecting on what you can do to follow the child, support them, make the environment more suitable for them, or what you need to discuss with their family. Keep your observations for future reference. You may find it beneficial to schedule a time (weekly, monthly, termly, etc.) to reflect on observations and discuss with others to make note of development and support your planning moving forward.

Box 3.3 Visitor Observation Example

Welcoming visitors (parents, carers, grandparents, professionals) to observe is a wonderful way to welcome the community into your setting. Your role is still to protect the child's work, so setting guidelines will help you do that.

Summary

To follow the child, you observe the child!

Incorporating effective observation throughout your setting will not only enhance your knowledge of the children but also support you in preparing an environment that meets the needs of the children. Observation is not just a tool used within your early year's environment but also a cornerstone of understanding children's development and guiding their learning experiences effectively.

This chapter has covered key points such as the following:

- The purpose of observation
- The art of observation
- Types of observations
- Skills for observation
- Utilising your observations

By honing your observational skills, you can truly follow the child and unlock the potential of each child's unique developmental journey.

Welcome to Garden City Montessori.

We are pleased to invite you into the children's environment. As a guest of the children, we ask that you please take a moment to read the following guidelines. They will assist you in understanding the Montessori environment, provide you with the information to have an enriching observation experience, and allow the children to work within their environment undisturbed.

OVERVIEW

The environments are orderly and beautiful and truly belongs to the children in it. They are responsible for, and take pride in, maintaining the room, working with the materials in a careful and thoughtful manner.

OBSERVATION GUIDELINES

PLEASE, TURN OFF ALL CELL PHONES BEFORE ENTERING THE SCHOOL

- Please plan to observe for a period of 45 minutes to 1 hour.
- A chair will be provided for you. It gives you a good vantage point into our environment. In order to see the environment as it normally operates, it is important to remain as unobtrusive and quiet around the children as possible.
- Children are naturally curious and may engage a visitor in conversation. A simple "hello" is acceptable. If they are persistent, smile and quietly let them know that you are there to watch them work, for example " I am here to observe you and your friends work.". If you have a pen and paper for jotting down notes, you may also tell them, "this is my work, I am here to watch children work." Please do not encourage conversation.
- If you are observing your own child, they may become shy, try to "perform" for you or seem to act in a silly or other unusual way. They may also become possessive of your attention. This is completely normal. For this reason, try not to compare your child with other children during your observation. Just smile and then remind your child that you are an observer today and you can see them from where you are sitting.
- Please respect the children's confidentiality and do not discuss individuals and their behaviours with other parents.
- Kindly remember that the *Guide's responsibility is with the children*. Please make a written note of any questions or comments as they arise. You may discuss your questions with the administrator or during your parent teacher conference.

RELAX AND ENJOY YOUR VISIT!

Figure 3.2 Example of Visitor Observation Guidelines

32 Observation

Figure 3.3 Observation

Figure 3.4 Observe

Observation 33

Figure 3.5 Guide

Figure 3.6 Step Aside

4 The Planes of Development and the Absorbent Mind

> **Box 4.1 Chapter Objective**
>
> By the end of this chapter, you will be able to do the following:
>
> - Understand what is meant by the term "absorbent mind" and the importance of the first six years of life.
> - Understand the plane of development in which the absorbent mind sits.
> - Identify the characteristics and stages of the absorbent mind.
> - Understand the relationship between the absorbent mind, the child, the adult, and the prepared environment.
> - Appreciate and value your role as the facilitator in supporting a child's absorbent mind.

Introduction

Dr. Maria Montessori's concept of the absorbent mind stands as a cornerstone of her pioneering pedagogy. Montessori championed for the recognition of the remarkable capacity of young children to effortlessly absorb knowledge from their environment, shaping the foundation of their development and learning experiences. Through her observations of young children, Montessori recognised the absorbent mind as a powerful force that shapes early learning and lays the foundation for future growth and exploration.

> The absorbent mind welcomes everything, puts its hope in everything, accepts poverty equally with wealth, adopts any religion and the prejudices and habits of its countrymen, incarnating all in itself. This is the child!
>
> (Montessori, 1964, The Absorbent Mind)

At the heart of Montessori's concept of the absorbent mind is the recognition of children as active, curious learners who possess the innate drive to explore and make sense of the world around them. From birth to approximately 6 years of age, children have a remarkable ability to absorb information from their environment with ease. The period, often referred to as the "sensitive period" (more on this in Chapter 5), is characterised by intense curiosity, rapid cognitive development, and a profound drive to learning.

The absorbent mind holds two distinct phases: the unconscious absorbent mind, which spans from birth to approximately 3 years of age, and the conscious absorbent mind, which extends from approximately 3 years to 6 years of age. During the unconscious absorbent mind phase, Montessori explained that children absorb information effortlessly and unconsciously. During this phase, children have the innate capacity to absorb impressions from their environment without conscious effort, shaping their foundation for future learning.

As children transition into the conscious absorbent mind phase, they become increasingly aware of their environment and actively engage in purposeful exploration and discovery. This phase is characterised by a heightened sense of curiosity, creativity, and independence, as children are eager to explore their surroundings, experiment with new concepts, and construct their understanding of the world through hands-on exploration and discovery.

Central to Montessori's concept of the absorbent mind is the recognition of the critical role played by the environment in which the children are in. Montessori explained the environment should support the children's natural inclination to learn. Montessori emphasised that environments should be carefully designed to provide rich, stimulating experiences that captivate children's interest and foster their curiosity. From the careful consideration on the materials/resources that invite a hands-on experience for the children to curated learning environments that promote independence and autonomy, environments should be crafted to support the absorbent mind and lifelong love of learning.

> The only thing the absorbent mind needs is the life of the individual; give him life and an environment and he will absorb all that is in it.
> (Montessori, 1946, London Lectures)

The Planes of Development

> I have found that in his development, the child passes through certain phases, each of which has its own particular needs. The characteristics of each plane are so different that the passages from one phase to another have been described by certain psychologists as "rebirths."
> (Montessori, 1971, The Four Planes of Education)

Montessori discovered there are periods of growth that every child goes through, and she called these the planes of development. These planes are sometimes referred to as the psychic phases or psychic planes. Montessori identified these as follows:

- 0–6 years old: Plane of the Absorbent Mind or Plane of the Sensorial Learner
- 6–12 years old: Period of Abstract Learner or Cosmic Education and/or Childhood
- 12–18 years old: Adolescence or ErdKinder (Children of the Earth)
- 18–24 years old: Plane of Selflessness/Selfhood or Adulthood

Montessori believed that education should acknowledge the difference between each plane and provide appropriate environments to support the needs of that plane. Although each plane has diverse needs to be met, there are some commonalities of all the planes:

- Each move from one plane to another is like a rebirth/metamorphosis, in that the entire organism changes.
- The needs and behaviours of each plane are quite distinct.
- To whatever extent the prior plane reaches completeness that is when they move on to the next plane.
- Whatever normalities or abnormalities occur in one plane, this will directly affect what happened in the next plane.

0–6 years: Plane of the Absorbent Mind or Plane of the Sensorial Learner.

The 0–6 child's needs are unconscious. They do not think about what they want; they are just driven to it. They are dependent on the adults in their environment for the basic human needs of food and shelter. Aside from those basic needs, the following are additional needs of the child:

- Warmth, love, and protection
- Connection with others (acceptance)
- A sense of security
- Order – to understand the outside world and feel order within themselves. To achieve this, they will absorb the outside order of the environment.
- Independence (on an increasing scale through this plane) – from the moment of birth when they become their own organism that must function on its own.
- Freedom: freedom to follow an inner guide. Only through freedom will the child learn how to behave.
- A rich and stimulating sensorial environment.
- To be exposed to culture by being with the people around them (celebrations, food, dress, religious practice).
- Need for spontaneity; to respond to what they are feeling.

Some manifestations of the 0–6 child:

- There is a phenomenally rapid physical growth.
- The child takes in information sensorially.
- They are very active and are often refreshed by activity. This drive to move is unconscious. This is good for the child because physical activity means brain activity is also happening.
- They have a preference to work vs play. They wish to be participating in the life of adults in the environment.
- Prefer purposeful activity. Real work.
- Intelligence grows very rapidly and is done so unconsciously, without conscious effort. The child simply absorbs their world around them.

There are two further planes within the absorbent mind plane that Montessori identified:

0–3 years old: the unconscious absorbent mind
3–6 years old: the conscious absorbent mind

During the 0–3 plane, the following points are significant:

- It is the time of greatest brain growth.
- An adult cannot directly approach the child, cannot tell them what to do, but must show them.
- The creation of faculties will be consolidated in the 3–6 plane: mind, personality, and spirit.
- It is also called the period of the spiritual embryo.

During the 3–6 plane, the following points are significant:

- The faculties are consolidated: mind, personality, and spirit.
- It is also called the period of the social embryo (creating the possibility to be social).
- Most of what the children do in this plane is unconscious, but in this plane, they begin to make conscious choices.

If we know that these planes exist and we have some ideas regarding the needs/characteristics of this child, then we need to make education fit the child. For education to be successful during the absorbent mind plane, the following should happen:

- There should be some choices afforded to the child from some acceptable options.
- Education should always consist of something for the mind and something for the body so there is a psychosomatic connection between the two.
- Allow the child to participate in purposeful activity.

The Spiritual Embryo *Important to Note the Word Spiritual Here Implies the Psychology of the Child

Montessori believed that a child's education should begin at birth. Consider the length of time it takes newborns to develop physically when other animals can walk, run, and communicate in a fraction of the time it takes humans to do the same. Montessori believed that this was because every individual had their own creative spirit, and these movements are voluntary, not instinctual. The child forms themselves, developing as a person through the absorption of their environment.

The child will absorb their environment in its entirety, the good and the bad. Montessori highlighted that the child does not have the capacity to absorb the bad and change it to good nor is the child able to refuse the absorption of good and bad (i.e., a sponge will soak up dirty or clean water – whatever is there.) The child's mind is like a sponge in that will take in whatever is presented to them. This first period of life is so important that we must look after the newborn's mental health as well as their other needs. We need to be aware of what we are offering the child.

> The child is specially favoured. He observes everything in sight, and experience shows that he absorbs it all equally. . . . He does not absorb only the mechanical camera of his eye, but a kind of psychochemical reaction is produced in him, so that these impressions become an integral part of his personality.
> (Montessori, 1949, The Absorbent Mind)

The child takes in many images during the absorbent mind stage, and the following are some of what the child absorbs:

- Relationships – between people, people and animals, water to sand, trees to leaves, etc.
- Deep-seated feelings – religion, attitudes, patriotism, racism, etc.
- Unstated feelings towards them – love, hate, like, dislike, frustration, etc.
- Qualities – shape, size, texture, smell, sound, etc.
- Language(s) – one, two, three, different ones, bad language, scientific language, any kind.
- Movement – walking fast or slow, seen movement, practiced movement, etc.
- Order – whatever is most consistent, must explore order to understand it.
- Anything in the environment.

When children are preverbal, they take their cues from body language, tone of voice, and facial expressions. Children at this stage are not logical, yet they are emotionally and physically connected to the world and, therefore, begin their relationship journey with people and their environment.

The Absorbent Mind and The Child

> There is in the child a special kind of sensitivity which leads him to absorb everything about him and it is this work of observing and absorbing that alone enables him to adapt himself to life. He does it in virtue of an unconscious power that exists in childhood. . . . The first period of the child's life is one of adaptation.
> (Montessori, 1967, The Absorbent Mind)

Understanding the Unconscious Absorbent Mind

Dr. Montessori compared this phase to a sponge-like mind, where children eagerly and effortlessly soak up impressions from their environment. During this period, children are particularly attuned to sensory experiences and environmental stimuli. They absorb language, social norms, cultural practices, and basic concepts such as order and sequence effortlessly, without the need for any formal instruction. Take language, a bilingual or multilingual child not only learns how to understand and speak a different language at a very young age but they also do this unconsciously and can also switch languages naturally based on who they are talking to! For most neurotypical children, you don't have to teach a child their native language; they absorb it by being exposed to it in their environment. It is the same for walking!

> The only thing the absorbent mind needs is the life of the individual; give him life and an environment and he will absorb all that is in it.
> (Montessori, 1946, London Lectures)

Key features of the unconscious absorbent mind:

1. Sensory sensitivity
2. Language acquisition
3. Order and sequence
4. Movement and exploration

Understanding the Conscious Absorbent Mind

During this period, children undergo a remarkable shift in their cognitive and developmental capacities. Unlike the unconscious absorbent mind, where learning occurs primarily through unconscious absorption of sensory experiences, the conscious absorbent mind is marked by a heightened awareness and purposeful engagement with the environment.

Children are increasingly aware of their surroundings and actively seek out opportunities for exploration and discovery. They demonstrate a keen interest in understanding their world, how it works, making connections, asking questions, and engaging in activities that serve their curiosity and interest.

Key features of the conscious absorbent mind:

1. Curiosity and enquiry
2. Purposeful exploration
3. Creativity
4. Independence and autonomy

The Absorbent Mind and the Role of the Adult

Consider your role as the facilitator of learning and create an environment that encourages children to follow their interests and explore at their own pace. Observation is key to understanding the children's interest and how you can best facilitate their growth. As children are constantly absorbing the information around them and learning from their environment, it is vitally important that careful consideration is given to what we expose them to. We help our children by being positive role models and setting good examples.

Although this responsibility can be immense to consider, we are creating a foundation for future personality. Traits and beliefs are being constructed. As parents, carers, and educators, it is our responsibility to help and support children along their journey.

1. Be aware of the capability of the absorbent mind – understand that the child is learning and absorbing **ALL** that their environment has to offer **ALL** the time. The child never stops learning. It is a natural process. We need to provide the optimal environment, the space and time to do their work and not get so focused on "filling" each passing moment.
2. Be aware of what you are modelling – it can be overwhelming to think that the child is absorbing all you do and say, even when we would rather they didn't! We need to be aware of our interaction with others, the environment, and of course, how we look after ourselves.
3. Offer hands-on experiences – whenever possible, offer the child the opportunity to explore with their senses. Through hands-on experiences, children will develop confidence, resilience, critical and creative thinking, problem solving, and autonomy, along with the child's emotional and physical development.
4. Exposure to the wonders of the world (real life) – Montessori is the real world! We live in a world of change, and to help prepare children for a future that is yet to be, we need to offer them the reality of today. Children are capable of so much and are full of potential.
5. Observe – do not rush the life of a child. Sit back and observe their learning in action. Value the role observation plays in supporting the child and ensuring you have all you need to meet their needs. Observation is key to understanding the child and what they have absorbed, and it gives you an insight into the interests of the child and where you might need to model more for the child.

6. Language exposure – from the beginning, use accurate language with the child. There is no need to "dumb down" our language. Use it, explain it, and allow your child to explore with it. Expose the child to the spoken word in the context of everyday life. Promote rich vocabulary and grammatically correct use of language.

Absorbent Mind and the Prepared Environment

According to Montessori, the relationship between the prepared environment and the absorbent mind is deeply intertwined and fundamental to the holistic development of the child. Montessori was clear that the environment for our young child immediately after birth must not be harsh, as it is the first experience after the safe and secure surroundings of the womb.

> There must not be too much contrast, as regards to warmth, light, noise with his conditions before birth, where in his mother's womb, there was perfect silence, darkness and an even temperature.
> (Montessori, 1964, The Absorbent Mind)

Montessori highlighted that whilst the newborn child may be unable to care for themselves, they are active seekers in understanding their environment, and they do this through their sensorial experience with their environment. The prepared environment plays a pivotal role in supporting and nurturing the absorbent mind during the critical early years of a child's development.

The environment, be it at home, childminders, nursery, or preschool, should be meticulously designed to provide a rich array of sensory experiences, hands-on learning opportunities, and age-appropriate materials/resources/activities that captivate the child's interest, meet their developmental needs, and facilitate their natural desire to learn. From the layout of the space to the selection of the materials/activities, every aspect needs to be carefully considered and carefully curated to meet the child's needs and support their exploration and discovery and aid in the journey to independence.

With its immense capacity to effortlessly absorb knowledge from the environment, the absorbent mind thrives in prepared environments. The supportive environment engages the children's senses, sparks their curiosity, and fosters their natural desire to learn.

Box 4.2 Case Study

Alex's morning at nursery (non-Montessori nursery). This case study shares the partial analysis of an observation on a morning routine for a 3-year-old. I share this one here, as it is from a more traditional early years setting but one that was at the beginning stages of implementing

Montessori principles and wanting to work on linking their new knowledge to their observations.

Alex is 3 years of age and attending a traditional early years' setting. Alex is greeted by his teacher upon arrival and joins his peers in a bustling space filled with toys, books, and learning resources. Alex's early years environment has designated play areas and mostly teacher-led activities.

During free play, Alex gravitates to the building blocks, and with enthusiasm, he begins to construct elaborate towers and structures, experimenting with balance, symmetry, and spatial relationships. Through this hands-on experience, Alex engages with his senses and develops foundation skills in STEM (science, technology, engineering, and mathematics).

During circle time, Alex participates in the teacher-led activities. He listens attentively, and the teacher reads a story, captivated by the colourful illustrations and engaging narrative. Through storytelling and the discussions that followed, Alex absorbs new vocabulary, concepts, and social skills, laying the groundwork for language development and social-emotional learning.

When playing outside, Alex explored the natural world, exploring insects, plants, and other wonders of the outdoor environment. He engages in play where he pretends to be a scientist exploring a jungle or an adventurer embarking on a quest. Through this outdoor exploration, Alex develops a sense of wonder, curiosity, and connection to the world around him.

Through Alex's experience on this day, we can recognise the principles of the absorbent mind in action. Alex's innate curiosity, creativity, and receptivity to learning through his interactions and activities are evident.

By providing a rich and stimulating environment filled with diverse experiences, Alex's environment lays the foundation for a lifetime of learning, growth, and discovery. The adults working with Alex begin to recognise the absorbent mind in action and how, in every interaction with his environment, Alex is growing and learning.

Summary

Understanding that the child goes through different planes of development is necessary to fully understand the needs of the child. During the first six years, the child is in the first plane of development, which Montessori stated was the absorbent mind phase. The absorbent mind is of the upmost importance in the early years of a child's development due to its pivotal role in shaping the foundation of learning, character formation, and overall wellbeing. Montessori identified the innate ability to absorb information from the environment, and this lays the foundation for all future learning experiences in which further knowledge and skills can be built upon.

The importance of this period between birth and 6 years of age requires acknowledgement from all adults who care for or work with young children. The unique period of sensitivity represents a critical window of opportunity for optimal learning and development. Children during this period possess an extraordinary capacity to absorb from their environments with ease and sensitivity. This allows children to acquire language, cultural norms, social skills, and other fundamental concepts effortlessly.

Montessori believed that the absorbent mind not only facilitates the acquisition of academic knowledge but also plays a crucial role in the formation of habits, attitudes, and character traits, and children not only absorb information but also social norms, cultural values, and emotional responses from their environments.

Through the relationship with the child's prepared environment, children during this period develop vital foundational skills such as concentration, coordination, independence, and self-regulation. This highlights the importance of a supportive environment that allows children to engage in purposeful activities and develop essential life skills autonomously. Recognising and nurturing the absorbent mind period is essential for providing children with a strong foundation for future academic success, personal fulfilment, and lifelong learning.

5 The Sensitive Periods

> **Box 5.1 Chapter Overview**
>
> By the end of this chapter, you will be able to do the following:
>
> - Understand what is meant by sensitive periods and the importance of these periods in a child's development.
> - Reflect on your approach to observation of the child to understand the sensitive periods.
> - Be confident in your response to the child's sensitive periods.
> - Consider the long-term impact the sensitive periods have on the overall development of the child.

Introduction

Maria Montessori identified a series of windows of opportunity known as "sensitive periods." These periods represent critical phases during which children exhibit an intense focus and receptivity to specific developmental milestones. Understanding these sensitive periods is paramount in Montessori education, as they provide valuable insights into the child's evolving needs, interest, and abilities. Montessori believed the most important sensitive periods of a child's life occurred between birth and age 6.

> A sensitive period refers to a special sensitivity which a creature acquires in its infantile state, while it is still in a proves of evolution. It is a transient disposition and limited to the acquisition of a particular trait. Once this trait, or characteristic, has been acquired, this special sensitivity disappears.
>
> (Montessori, 1977, The Secret of Childhood)

Maria Montessori observed that children undergo periods of heightened sensitivity and receptivity to certain stimuli during their early years. These sensitive periods are characterised by an intense focus, a natural inclination towards specific activities, and rapid skill acquisition in particular areas of development. Montessori emphasised the importance of educators, parents, and caregivers to comprehend the intense or, at times, peculiar behaviour and actions of the child to interpret what sensitive period the child was in.

> At such a time everything is easy; all is life and enthusiasm. Every effort marks an increase in power. Only when the goal has been obtained does fatigue and the weight of indifference come on. When one of these psychic passions is exhausted another area is enkindled. Childhood thus passes from conquest to conquest in a constant rhythm that constitutes its joy and happiness.
> (Montessori, 1977, The Secret of Childhood)

Montessori originally observed the following sensitive periods:

- Language
- Small objects
- Grace and courtesy
- Order
- Music
- Movement
- Refinement of senses
- Numbers
- Wellbeing

It is important to recognise that others appear as the child gets older, but even more have been identified since Montessori's original observations.

> The most important period of life is not the age of university studies, but the first one, the period from birth to six.
> (Montessori, 1967, The Absorbent Mind)

Sensitive Periods and the Child

The child will demonstrate several possible characteristics when they are in a sensitive period, such as the following:

- Mimicking
- Prolonged concentration periods
- Outburst of behaviour (often known as tantrums)

- Repetition of activity/task
- Dislike to disruptions or removal from activity or task

For the benefit of awareness, the focus will be on the following sensitive periods.

- Movement
- Language
- Refinement of senses
- Order

Sensitive Period for Movement – 0–3 Years of Age and The Refinement of Movement to 5 Years of Age

Have you ever found yourself wondering where a child gets their energy from or just why they are unable to be still? Or why the child is wanting to go up and down steps repeatedly?

It may be a sensitive period!

Some signs that indicate the child is in a sensitive period for movement are as follows:

- The child is sensitive to how, when, and where people move, and they have a drive to acquire the same movement themselves.
- The child is sensitive to their own movements.
- The child is acutely aware of their own movements.

From birth to approximately 3 years of age, children are engaged with development of their gross motor skills (large body movements). When you consider a newborn baby is reliant on the adult to move them about and within a short period of time (sometimes within the year), the child learns to walk on their own! Refinement and coordination of movements begin around 2 ½ years to about 5 years.

In no other period of life will such physical development take place at such a fast pace. As the child reaches the end of this sensitive period for movement, the intense need to move starts to fade away, and you will observe the child's ability to sit for longer periods of time.

Sensitive Period for Language – From Birth to 6 (and Beyond) (Does tend to have a peak at around 2 years of age but this can vary a lot)

From before birth, the child is absorbing language from the environment around them (see Chapter 4). It is prime time to offer rich language to your child. This prenatal influence of language is important in the development of spoken language for the child. Children in the sensitive period of language have unlimited capacity for language.

Some signs that indicate the child is in a sensitive period for language are as follows:

- The child is passionate and in tune with the human voice/sound.
- The child does not care how difficult or simple the language is, they just want to hear it.

Offering a language-rich environment to the child is one of the simplest, most effective, and most inexpensive way to support a child's language development.

- Use real language – leave the baby talk behind and use a regular tone when speaking to the child. I know this can be a real struggle when immersed in infant gorgeousness! Speak in full sentences.
- Read – read often and then read some more! Offer a variety of books (picture/story/poetry/classic).
- Go explore the outdoors – describe what you see. The outdoors is filled with immense opportunities for language. Be descriptive and use that rich language.
- Sing – the wonderful thing here is children do not care what your singing sounds like; they just love that you are singing! Expose the child to different genres of music.

It is important to note here that the sensitive period for language does not mean it's the sensitive period for just English (mother tongue). Children can, without effort, embrace multiple language at this period of their lives, if the environment they are in is affording them the opportunities to do so.

Box 5.2 Reflective Consideration

If a family is multilingual, I do not recommend to only focus on one language. Be consistent in the approach, but offering more than one language will not hinder the develop of the mother tongue or desired language.

Sensitive Period for Refinement of Senses

The sensitive period of the refinement of senses is characterised by the child's fascination with sensorial experiences (touch, taste, smell, sound, sight).

> The senses, being explorers of the world, open the way to knowledge.
> (Montessori, 1949, The Absorbent Mind)

In a world that is busy and hectic, it can go against the grain to slow down and embrace the beauty of the world around us, rather than focusing on that end point/destination. To support the child with the refinement of their senses, we need to be patient and slow down.

At birth, the child is introduced to their senses, as this whole new world is now there for them to see, touch, taste, hear, and smell. In early infancy, this is how the child gathers information and builds their brain.

At around the age of 2, a child will begin to refine their senses. Everything calls to the young child. Reflect on the child who just wants to touch everything or put every object in their mouth! The child is biologically wired to take it all in.

Sensitive Period for Order

The sensitive period of order is defined by the child's intense interest in sorting out and categorising all their experiences. The child may demonstrate their interest in arranging and organising objects, and they are keen to understand the patterns and relationships. Children during this sensitive period are naturally drawn to activities such as sorting.

Children during this period are also in need of order and structure in their environment. They show their need to be cared for in a certain way (often like their primary caregiver), and they need consistency and routine. This can be highlighted in a child's dislike to change. Even the most minor change can result in emotional distress for the child. Providing order in the child's life helps them to feel secure and avoid them becoming disoriented. This is why the early years prepared environment is so important for the young child.

The Sensitive Periods and the Adult – Observing Sensitive Periods in Early Years

> Scientific observation then has established that education is not what the teacher gives; education is a natural process spontaneously carried out by the human individual and is acquired not by listening to words but by experiences upon the environment.
>
> (Montessori, 1963, Education for a New World)

Observation of the child's interests, movements, and behaviours are the first steps to identifying and recognising the sensitive period in a child. Observation is a fundamental aspect of the Montessori environment, and time needs to be given to develop observational skills for all adults in the environment. By observing a child in their prepared environment, adults can identify the sensitive period the child is experiencing and then plan and deliver activities that best meet their needs at that time.

During a sensitive period, children may demonstrate high levels of focus and concentration on a specific activity. They may be eager to repeat this activity to excess or demonstrate a strong interest in a particular topic/subject. Or the child may demonstrate frustration when not being given the opportunity that their mind and body is yearning to do.

Sensitive periods are not always in silo. Often, they overlap for a child. Recognising the sensitive periods in the child is the first aspect to supporting the child, but allowing the child to progress through their sensitive period at their own pace is another important aspect. It is through our observation that we will understand the child's needs. The sensitive periods are different for each child and will vary as the child grows and develops. Redirecting the child to another task will not change that inner drive the child has, but preparing ourselves and the environment to support the child's will will support that intrinsic drive.

> Man's mind does not spring from nothing; it is built up on the foundations laid by the child in his sensitive periods.
> (Montessori, 1972a, The Secret of Childhood)

Box 5.3 Reflective Activity

Think of a child in your setting that has recently shown a fascination with a particular activity or topic.

1. What did you observe? What characteristics was the child demonstrating?
2. Did the environment meet the child's need? If so, how do you know? If not, how do you know?
3. How did you respond?
4. Knowing what you know now about sensitive periods, what would you do differently, if at all, to support the child?

Sensitive Periods and the Prepared Environment

As we now know, during the sensitive period, the child is highly motivated to acquire a specific ability and is fanatical about achieving it. Montessori stated that the sensitive periods are a natural occurrence, albeit different for every child. She also recognised that once the sensitive period had passed, it does not occur again. This is why it is important for adults working with children to be prepared to support the child during this period.

The adult acts as a guide for the child; they follow the child's needs and interests, preparing an environment that supports their drive. The materials are hands-on, self-directed, and appropriate for the child's needs. The adult having observed the child in a sensitive period will be knowledgeable on what activities are necessary and suitable to support their current sensitive period.

The young child needs activities with purpose and meaning. The environment is not there to provide passive entertainment for the child but to ignite that internal drive and hunger for growth, knowledge, and development.

The principles of the prepared environment (see Chapter 6) support the child through their sensitive periods:

- Freedom – freedom to explore their interest, freedom of movement, and freedom of choice.
- Structure and order
- Beauty
- Social environment
- Intellectual environment
- Nature
- Hands-on
- Reality

The prepared environment should nourish the child's sensitive periods. The child is working hard to make sense of their world around them and rely on the order of their environments. If the order is unexpectedly altered, this can have a great impact of the child's sense of security. This can be a challenging time for adults, but observation (see Chapter 3) is needed more than frustration here. Observe to find out what the child needs and how to support them.

Summary

The sensitive periods are critical windows of opportunities during which children are naturally inclined to acquire specific skills and knowledge. Understanding and fostering these sensitive periods is key to optimising the learning experiences for the child.

The sensitive periods are phases children go through of intense focus and interest in a particular area of development, and Montessori observed that children go through these periods sequentially and at their own pace. The distinctive characteristics of the sensitive periods enable adults to observe these phases to support the child's learning and development.

There are various types of sensitive periods the child goes through, and it is through observation and understanding these stages that the adult can prepare the environment with appropriate activities and opportunities to facilitate the child's sensitive periods. The sensitive periods align with the child's natural development and support adults in fostering optimal learning experiences for the child.

6 The Prepared Environment

> **Box 6.1 Chapter Overview**
>
> By the end of this chapter, you will be able to do the following:
>
> - Understand the purpose and benefits of the prepared environment.
> - Explore the key features of the prepared environment.
> - Address the purpose of the area with an environment.
> - Understand the role of the adult in preparation of the environment.
> - Appreciate the importance of the outdoor environment

Introduction

Montessori recognised the fundamental necessity for careful preparation of the child's environment. The environment should provide the child with order, structure, beauty, reality, and simplicity, along with child-sized resources and furniture, all to enhance the child's independent functioning and learning opportunities. Everything the child comes to interact with within the environment needs careful consideration and thought to help stimulate the child's natural desire to learn and explore.

> When we speak of environment, we include the sum total of objects which a child can freely choose and use as he pleases, that is to say, according to his needs and tendencies. A teacher simply assists him at the beginning to get his bearings among so many different thigs and teaches him the precise use of them, that is to say, she introduces him to the ordered and active life of the environment. But then she leaves him free in the choice and execution of his work.
>
> (Montessori, 1972a, The Secret of Childhood)

Having already discussed the importance of the prepared environment for a child's development and wellbeing, this chapter will explore how Montessori emphasised on creating distinct areas within the environment to offer optimal learning for the child. Montessori believed the organisation of the environment can promote engagement, exploration, curiosity, independence, and autonomy. The prepared environment is a meaningful structured learning space that has been designed and organised to meet the needs of the children.

Children absorb what is around them, including their environment. Montessori believed that children use their early experiences to build the foundations of their minds, and these experiences come from the child's environments. Montessori emphasised the importance that everything the child encountered should facilitate and maximise independent learning and exploration. This preparation of the child's environment should appeal to the child's sensitive periods for learning as well as their fundamental needs.

Within the prepared environment, there will be a great deal of movement for the child, along with a range of opportunities for the child to explore and learn with the carefully prepared activities. The adult in this instance is the preparer and the communicator of the environment to the child and holds responsibility for maintaining the order of the prepared environment.

> The first aim of the prepared environment is, as far as possible, to render the growing child independent of the adult.
> (Montessori, 1972a, The Secret of Childhood)

The prepared environment is not merely a physical space; it is a dynamic ecosystem that nurtures the holistic development of the child. By providing the child with an environment that not only respects but also responds to the child's natural development trajectory, you are empowering the child to become independent lifelong learners, critical thinkers, and active participants in their own learning journey who become compassionate contributors to society.

Of course, this can only be accomplished by understanding the child's developmental needs and offering the activities that will support their development. It is important to remind ourselves that every child not only grows at their own pace but they are also unique in their interests and not all children will be interested in all activities within your environment! It is the role of the adult to use their observation to understand each child's interest and progress. This will enable the adult to be prepared to assist and support the child when needed. At times, it will be necessary to reconsider the layout of the environment and the activities offered within the environment. The children will let you know when they are not connecting with them.

There are three main components of the prepared environment (see Chapter 2):

1. The child
2. The adult
3. The environment itself

Objectives of a Prepared Environment

When preparing the environment for children, it is important to remember that the environment is for the child. It is not the adults' environment that the child must fit into; it is an environment for the child, and as mentioned earlier, the adults are the preparers of the environment, focusing on;

- Promoting independence
- Fostering concentration
- Supporting exploration and discovery
- Nurturing order and organisation
- Cultivating a sense of community

> When we say that children are free in our schools, organisation is necessary, and organisation more detailed than in other schools, so that the children may be free to work.
> (Montessori, 1967, The Absorbent Mind)

Principles of the Prepared Environment

- Freedom – freedom to explore and follow their own natural interest, impulses, and intrinsic desire to learn. This supports the development of their knowledge of the world around them and a sense of belonging. Within the prepared environment, children experience freedom of movement, exploration, social interaction, time, and self.
- Structure and order – the child needs order in their environment or the child is unable to make sense of their world. The organised environment provides children with the opportunity to focus on their work with peace and independence.
- Beauty – the beauty of the environment will offer the child a sensorial experience with their space and can bring a sense of calmness. This beauty is incorporated using natural materials, natural/soft lighting, and nature, all an inspiration for positive wellbeing and learning.
- Nature and reality – providing children with real-life experiences enhances their connection to their world and their understanding of the world. Children will develop a sense of respect, responsibility, and appreciation for the natural world.
- Social environment – although we recognise that children in early years are in the early stages of developing their social skills, the environment creates a community where they can learn these skills and have a sense of belonging.
- Intellectual environment – the activities in the environment support the curious mind of the child and meets their intrinsic motivation to learn and their developmental needs. The environment promotes the independent learning of the child through exploration and discovery with the hands-on opportunities.

54 The Prepared Environment

The child, by carrying out experiments in a prepared environment, perfects himself, but a certain amount of apparatus is then necessary, and space is necessary. Once the child has achieved concentration, he continues to be concentrated through many activities and as he becomes more and more active, the teacher becomes less and less so.

(Montessori, 1967, The Absorbent Mind)

Features of the Prepared Environment

- Structure and order
- Defined curriculum area
- Activities displayed in a progressive order
- Left-to-right progression
- Freedom of movement
- Freedom of choice
- Promotion of independence
- Freedom within limits

Figure 6.1 Examples of Prepared Environments

The Prepared Environment   55

Figure 6.2 Examples of Prepared Environments

Figure 6.3 Examples of Prepared Environments

Figure 6.4 Examples of Prepared Environments

The Prepared Environment and the Child

The child is the focus when preparing the environment at school, home, or wherever the child is spending quality time in. We now know the children in early years are in their absorbent mind stage, so the consideration of all aspects of the environment is necessary for the child to connect, grow, and develop within the environment.

Montessori recognised the importance of the environments we offer our children and how children can thrive within the right environments that foster independent learning, becoming fully immersed within the exploration and discovery of their own knowledge. Each child interacts with the curriculum areas, following their own interests, and needs, with activities that have been designed to stimulate and inspire interaction.

There are psychological aspects of the prepared environment that have an impact for the child:

1. Order: The physical and nonphysical order of the environment support the growing mental order of the child, enabling them to start to make sense of their world.
2. Freedom: Freedom of movement, freedom of exploration, freedom of voice, freedom of social development, and freedom of emotional development all lead to freedom of choice for the child.
3. Freedom within limits: Freedom occurs within the scope of limits that the child has been part of making and are aware of them. These limits also support the independence and freedom of choice of the child.

Children need their adults to know how to prepare the environment, when to connect the child to specific activities and skills, and when to step back and let the child develop and grow through their own exploration and independence within the environment.

The Prepared Environment and the Adult

The adult is the preparer of the environment for the child. The adult is the link between the child and their environment. As we know the needs of the child's absorbent mind, we understand that the child is developing cognitive habits, so we prepare an environment to reinforce those.

For the adult, besides the preparer of the physical environment, they are the guide, the observer, and their role is to know how best to prepare the environment and when to connect each child to the activities and skills offered in the environment.

> The children are now working as if I did not exist.
> (Montessori, 1967, The Absorbent Mind)

One of the fundamental aspects of the prepared environment is that it supports the child to be independent. The planning and design require careful consideration to foster this in the child. Again, we are reminded of the importance of observation here. It is through your observations you will know how the environment is serving the children.

Tips to consider as part of your role in a prepared environment:

1. Every day is a new day. Greet the child with love and genuine happiness to start a fresh day with them.
2. Follow the child! Observe often and be mindful of that urge to step in unnecessarily. Do not take the control away from the child.
3. Protect the child's work. Do not interrupt the child who is focused and concentrated. Save your questions for later.

4. Protect the lessons. When a child is being given a lesson, the other adults must protect that lesson from interference or interruption.
5. Model. Practice the behaviour you wish from the child. Practice the language you want the child to absorb (manners, questioning, etc.). Model how to be part of the community within the environment.
6. Respect. Treat everyone with respect. Ask permission of the child if you are going to touch their body (unless you need to for safety and then let them know what you are doing). Practice how to interrupt someone as you wish the children to interrupt you.
7. Listen. Actively listen to the child. Let them finish what they have to say and ask for clarity if you need to, but do not dismiss their emotions, concerns, and comments.
8. Reflect. Be reflective on your own practice and be ready to adapt and adjust when needed. Use your observation to help guide you on what is working and what is not. Reflect on situations for how to further support the child.
9. Learn. Continue to learn about the child, their needs, their interest, and how you can best meet their needs.
10. Enjoy. Celebrate the journey you are on with the children. Enjoy the small moments as well as the big ones. Show the child that you are genuinely happy to be with them.

Physical Aspects of the Prepared Environment

Our young children are developing their independence, and Montessori believed that the prepared environment could facilitate this when used and valued as a teacher. It is the interaction between the child and the environment that fosters the child's autonomy.

Within a Montessori environment, the space is divided into four distinct areas:

1. Practical life – practical life activities offer the child opportunities to learn and gain independence in care of self, care of others, care of the environment, social development, focus and concentration, hand-and-eye coordination, and grace and courtesy.
2. Sensorial – sensorial activities offer the child opportunities to discover the world through the development of their senses. The child explores size, colour, shape, texture, etc., developing the ability to classify, sort, and discriminate, whilst developing a foundation for language, geometry, and mathematics.
3. Language – language activities offer the child to acquire vocabulary and develop skills needed for writing and reading. With the use of hands-on materials, the child will learn letter sounds, how sounds together can make a word, and how the structure of words build a sentence. The child will also develop their skill of using a pencil.

4. Mathematics – math activities offer the child the opportunity to identify numerals and comprehend the connection between numeral and quantity. The child will gain understanding in place value and base-10 before moving to addition, subtraction, multiplication, and division. The hands-on experiences enable the child to explore to gain a firm understanding of mathematics and recognise mathematical patterns.

There are, of course, other aspects such as art, geography, etc., but mentioned earlier are the four main areas, and Montessori believed that having distinct curriculum areas within your environment aids the need for order and structure for the child, as well as giving them the freedom to completely develop through physical and sensorial stimulation.

Taking into consideration the earlier principles and aspects of the prepared environment, here are a few points to consider when developing the physical aspect of your environment:

1. Less is more – be a minimalist! Avoid the clutter or the overstimulation through unnecessary décor that can cause distraction and disruption.
2. Structure and order – think about the children and their needs. The environment should be structured and organised, where every activity has a place.
3. Child-size – the child should be able to interact with all that is in their environment independently. The resources, the activities, the shelves, and the furniture should all be accessible to the child.
4. Sensorial – the activities and the aesthetics of the environment should offer a sensorial experience for the child that promotes engagement.
5. Movement – the early years child needs to move! The space should provide freedom and independence to the child. Ensure the space is not cluttered and there is a positive movement flow within the environment.
6. Hands-on – activities for children to touch, feel, smell, taste, and see offer the child a concrete experience with the activity and learning. These hands-on experiences require reality for the child to understand their world.

The Outdoor Environment

Montessori saw the outdoors as an extension of the indoor environment. She believed that children should be free to move between both. Whilst that is not realistic for many settings today, it is still important to prioritise the opportunities being offered to the child to be outdoors.

Long before outdoor settings such as forest school were a thing, Montessori advocated for the connectiveness between outdoor and indoor environments. Don't get me wrong, I am a huge fan of forest schools today, and I recognise the challenges settings face in providing this connectiveness, but I urge settings to reflect on their current practice and see what changes they can make to bring nature to the children's learning experiences.

60 *The Prepared Environment*

Having a properly planned and prepared outdoor area allows the curriculum to go even further and come alive for the child. The space can offer a multifunctional space where activities can be explored with free movement between the indoor and outdoor. Outdoor should not be reserved just for free playtime (see Chapter 7).

> Education is a natural process spontaneously carried out by the human individual and is acquired not by listening to words but by experiences upon the environment.
> (Montessori, 1963, Education for a New World)

Figure 6.5 Outdoor Prepared Environments

The Prepared Environment 61

Figure 6.6 Outdoor Prepared Environments

Figure 6.7 Outdoor Prepared Environments

> **Box 6.2   Reflective Practice**
>
> Take a walk around your setting and note if there are any activities that would not be suitable for outdoors. If there are, ask yourself:
>
> - What is stopping this activity from being used outside? Can that be resolved?
> - What is the purpose of this activity?
> - Is this activity being used by the children?
> - What are your reservations for this work to be outdoors?
>
> There should be nothing that cannot be used outside with the right preparation of the space outdoors.

Summary

The prepared environment is designed to facilitate a child's independence, exploration, and self-directed learning, intentionally prepared by the adult to support the child's development and foster their natural curiosity and innate drive to learn.

By embracing the principles of the prepared environment, adults are equipped with the knowledge and understanding of the importance of the environment, and through observation of the child, the adult will begin to understand how to prepare an environment that promotes and fosters independence, freedom, order, beauty, and emotional development as well as serve the intellectual development of the child.

7 Play Is Work

> **Box 7.1   Chapter Objectives**
>
> By the end of this chapter, you will be able to do the following:
>
> - Understand the value of play in early childhood and how the child views their play.
> - Identify the links between the absorbent mind, sensitive periods, and play.
> - Understand the importance of the child's agency in their own play.
> - Be confident in your role as the adult supporting a child's play.

Play is a very misused adult word. To a child it is a way of life. To an adult it often means unimportant recreational things we do when we are not working.
— Jean-Jaques Rousseau

Introduction

The United Nations Conventions on the Rights of the Child articulated the right to play for all children (Article 31, UNCRC, 1989), but "play" is a complex term and often interpretated differently amongst adults. As adults, we often consider play as a simple source of entertainment that occupies a child's time. Play is more than what children do when they aren't "working" or what they do in their free time/break time. The play-learning dichotomy trivialises play as an activity for break time or as a reward for when the "real" work is completed. However, Montessori believed that play is in fact the work of the child and believed it was through play that the child became a learner. She also highlighted that play is learning for the child, and it allows exploration of self and of others. Children play to understand the world around them and is a fundamental aspect of their growth and development and should be encouraged and embraced for the crucial role it plays in the developing child.

Montessori was influential in her vision to combine play with learning and believed this satisfied the child's curiosity and playfulness at the same time. Montessori was aware of the importance psychologists were putting on play, but she often challenged their views, as through her own observations, she revealed that given the choice between toys and carefully prepared activities/materials, the children rarely chose the toys. The toys were trivial in comparison to the purposeful and engaging materials offered.

In the early childhood world, there are various types of play but also various definitions or interpretations of play. This itself can lead to very different experience for children. We somewhat lose the meaning of play when we try to label and restrict what play is for the child. Play should be valued as an intrinsic activity that enhances creativity, social and emotional development as well as academic. When play is guided by the child's natural development and interest, this can lead to deep and purposeful concentration and focus and meaningful experiences. Montessori's idea of all purposefully prepared activities for a child can be considered play when the child is choosing their activity freely.

> There is an age when children play; we call it the age of play. But what is play if not to do those things which entail the movement of the hands? Children need to touch, to move all the things which they find in the environment.
> (Montessori, The 1946 London Lectures)

Play can be any of the following:

- Fun
- Quiet
- Challenging
- Engaging
- Purposeful
- Serious
- Exploration and discovery
- Freedom
- Engagement of senses
- Self-directed
- Directed
- Imagination
- Creativity
- Social
- Individual
- Spontaneous
- Voluntary

I am sure you can add to the previous list from your own perspective, but we focus on these few examples of what play can be and start to consider what that can mean for the child.

Understanding Play

The basic definition of play does not help with this understanding, as according to the Oxford dictionary, play is to engage in activity for enjoyment and recreation rather than serious or practical purposes. Despite the vast research that describes play as fundamental to early childhood development and a natural way of learning, play is often undervalued and misunderstood within our settings.

Montessori believed that play and learning go hand in hand and was instrumental in her vision to combine play with learning, as she believed this satisfied the child's curiosity and playfulness at the same time. Montessori was aware of the importance psychologists were putting on play, but Montessori challenged this view of play, as mentioned earlier, it was through her observations of children that it was revealed, given a choice between toys and the prepared materials offered, children rarely chose the toys.

> Psychologists have attached great importance to [play] and make vague statements – that children play at this age – that they develop their character through play. They also say that the individuality of the children is revealed through play.
> (Montessori, 1946, The London Lectures)

Montessori believed the purposeful and engaging materials offered more to the child and children felt they were doing something of importance and value when using the prepared materials. Montessori also argued that in the right environment, a child's work will bring them higher affect, energy, and intrinsic motivation.

Play and the Child

Play is a natural classroom for children, where exploration and experimentation occurs freely, and children will learn through hands-on experiences.

> The hands are the instrument of a man's intelligence.
> (Montessori, 1949, The Absorbent Mind)

As discussed in Chapter 4, the absorbent mind of a child means the child is taking in all their environment has to offer. They are learning from what is around them, and Montessori expressed the need for the child to learn through real-life experiences but in a fun way. Play should be an integral part of every early childhood environment.

Within a typical Montessori environment, you won't see "dress-up games." Instead, you will see children engaging with learning about real-life situations in an engaging way. That does not mean there is no place for the opportunity to "dress up" in an early year's environment if you are incorporating Montessori principles; it means it should be a purposeful learning opportunity that can then lead to exploration directed by the child's own interest and need.

Play is considered a process for the child. The activities that have been offered to the child are available, as they serve a purposeful purpose for the child and not to serve as a goal set by the adults that the child must reach. If we focus on Montessori's view that "play is the work of the child," we should start to consider the activities, toys, or materials we offer the child as tools to their learning. They will learn about the world around them through these tools and develop skills, such as the following:

1. Decision making
2. Critical thinking
3. Creative thinking
4. Motor development
5. Muscle control and strength
6. Exploration
7. Problem solving
8. Collaboration with others
9. Social skills
10. Motivation

Children learn through experiences, and part of that is the hands-on experience. Encouraging children to explore the world around them through exploration involves the child touching and experimenting (playing) with activities. Referring to the child's sensitive periods (Chapter 5), we know this period is indicated by the child wanting to explore the world through their senses; this is done through the real-life experiences being offered to the child within the prepared environment.

> The strength of even the smallest children is more than we imagine, but it must have a free play in order to reveal itself.
> (Montessori, 1972b, The Discovery of the Child)

Play and the Role of the Adult

Montessori considered it the role of the adult to keep the "fire" of learning alive in young children, and the interactions adults have with children have a great impact on extending their learning. Adults are instrumental in fostering a positive learning experience and promoting social and emotional development for child. Whilst it is necessary to build on this adult-child relationship, it is necessary for the adult to engage with supporting the child's independence and autonomy throughout their early childhood.

Box 7.2 Reflective Question

Where do you place yourself in the child's work?
As the adult in the setting, are you the lead, the facilitator, the coworker, or the intruder?

Whilst play is the work of the child, adults do have the responsibility to prepare the environment for the child to "play" in. Quality play experiences are achieved when adults participate, but it is important to know the difference between the adult controlling and the adult supporting. Montessori believed that the environment itself would teach the child, but it is the adult that organises the space, the activities, and the opportunities for the child. Montessori also emphasised the importance of the adult remaining the quiet observer whilst the child is engaged in the environment; she also expressed the need for the adult to have a period of preparation of self and to not impose themselves into the work of the child.

It is after the observation of the child and assessing the child's need that the adult can fully prepare an effective environment. The environment should be secure and safe but offer enough freedom of choice and opportunities for engagement through activities that meet the developing needs of the child. That observation (see Chapter 3) should be viewed as the opportunity to ask the question: "How can I support the child to learn and grow?"

Another important aspect of an adult's role is the language they use when interacting with the children. When play is co-constructed between the child and the adult, the influence of the adult is less likely to impact the perception of play and non-play activities and, in return, will allow the child's natural playful approach to be valued and respected.

Work Needs Play!

Montessori found that children prefer to work rather than play (how adults view play).

> A child who concentrates is immensely happy.
> (Montessori, 1949, The Absorbent Mind)

A misconception on what Montessori meant when she said "play is the work of the child" is still present today. For some, they believe Montessori forces children to work with the exclusion of creativity or self-expression (play), and this couldn't be further from the truth. Montessori recognised that children are naturally more drawn to towards reality-based activities than traditional toys, and this is why real-life opportunities are encouraged for young children.

The activities offered to the young child should spark creativity, exploration, and play, and this is what Montessori considered when creating her materials for the environment. It is the adult's definition of play that work is something we must do so that we can have fun doing something else. Montessori was intentional using the term "work," as she had immense respect for the child's activity and wanted to acknowledge the profound psychological, emotional, and physical development the child was experiencing.

The young child's work is internal and without regard for external goals or results. It is that learning process that Montessori referred to as work as it is great work and takes work to grow!

> It is certain that the child's attitude towards work represents a vital instinct; for without work his personality cannot organise itself and deviates from the normal lines of its construction. Man builds himself through working. Nothing can take the place of work, neither physical well-being nor affection, and, on the other hand, deviations cannot be corrected by either punishment or example.
> (Montessori, 1977, The Secret of Childhood)

Play is the child's work of self-construction.

Play and the Prepared Environment

The activities provided to the children in your early years setting are carefully considered and prepared to develop specific skills. They are not just toys you leave out for the child; they are tools for learning. Each activity serves a purpose (indirect and/or direct), such as focus and concentration, motor development, social skills, etc. Activities that offer:

- Empowerment
- Self-directed activity
- Sensorial
- Exploration
- Social development
- Motor development
- Concentration and focus

Children thrive in environments that are purposeful and offer routine, structure, safety, and security. Learning should not be forced or rushed, and children should be free to pursue their interest in an environment that they are trusted in to engage in meaningful work. Children have a need for both structured and unstructured work, and Montessori recognised children as capable thinkers, doers, creators, and learners.

The prepared environment, ready for the child, needs consideration for the needs of the child. We need to rid ourselves and the environment of adding

Figure 7.1 Play in the Prepared Environment; Play Is the Work the Child Does

Figure 7.2 Play in the Prepared Environment; Play Is the Work the Child Does

70 *Play Is Work*

Figure 7.3 Play in the Prepared Environment; Play Is the Work the Child Does

the pressure of our expectations of what is meaningful work and what isn't. It is through our observations and purposeful engagement that we begin to understand the drive of the child.

Provide the environment, the opportunities, the guidance, and the activities, but ultimately, follow the child.

Outdoor Play

> Let the children be free; encourage them; let them run outside when it is raining; let them remove their shoes when they find a puddle of water; and when the grass of the meadows is wet with dew, let them run on it and trample it with their bare feet; let them rest peacefully when a tree invites them to sleep beneath its shade; let them shout and laugh when the sun wakes them in the morning.
>
> (Montessori, 1972b, The Discovery of the Child)

Montessori believed that the outdoor environment is a natural extension of the classroom where children can continue to build knowledge through sensorial experience with nature and the natural environment. Playing outside is more than a time to burn off energy or take a break from the work the child has been doing. It is a vital aspect of a child's development. Working outside allows children to explore with their senses, fostering scientific enquiry and inspiring creativity. It also aids in the development of the following:

- Physical development
- Social and emotional development
- Cognitive development
- Independence
- Self-confidence
- Critical thinking
- Problem solving

Too often, we are seeing time outdoors being taken away from children for more time with directed instruction indoors. This is having a negative impact on children's development. Every setting can pledge to be outdoors more and incorporate it into their curriculum. Young children are in that absorbent mind phase in which they are soaking up information through their senses. Offering rich opportunities in the outdoor environment where the children can use their senses will support their development.

Examples of activities:

- Nature walks
- Outdoor exploration
- Gardening (flowers, herbs, vegetables)
- Caring for animals
- Unstructured outdoor play
- Work outside
- Eat outside!
- Just sit outdoors
- Sweeping a path
- Pouring water through funnels
- Washing windows
- Filling the birdfeeder
- Digging in sand
- Hammering nails into tree stump
- Crayon rubbings of a bark of a tree
- Leaf rubbings
- Mud kitchen
- Cloud spotting
- Read outside

72 *Play Is Work*

Outdoor education is an opportunity for children to develop their appreciation for nature. Montessori emphasised the power of the natural learning environment and argued children should have free access to the outdoors, with no separation between the indoor and outdoor learning environment.

> There must be provision for the child to have contact with nature; to understand and appreciate the order, the harmony and the beauty in nature.
>
> (Montessori, 1972a, The Secret of Childhood)

Figure 7.4 Play Outdoors Is the Work of the Child

Figure 7.5 Play Outdoors Is the Work of the Child

Figure 7.6 Play Outdoors Is the Work of the Child

> **Box 7.3 Note About the Weather!**
>
> There is an old quote that says "There is no such thing as bad weather, only unsuitable clothing" which should be remembered in all settings working with children. The weather, rain, snow, or other simply come part of the prepared environment! Children will need their outdoor clothing for all seasons, but most importantly, the adult must be mindful not to instil any of their own feelings towards a particular weather. Keep language neutral and descriptive.

There is no description, no image in any book that is capable of replacing the sight of real trees, and all the life to be found around them, in a real forest. Something emanates from those trees which speaks to the soul, something no book, no museum is capable of giving.
(Montessori, 1996, From Childhood to Adolescence)

United Nations Rights of the Child

I couldn't let this chapter go without writing about the United Nations Convention on the Rights of the Child (UNCRC). It is an international human rights treaty that grants all children and young people a comprehensive set of rights. There are 54 Articles that make up the UNCRC, and Article 31 states that children have a right to have fun in a way that they want to and have age-appropriate activities available to them, but children should be able to engage freely.

The UNCRC recognises that play is not just a "leisure" activity but a crucial part of a child's development, contributing to the physical, social, cognitive, and emotional wellbeing of a child. The UNCRC, recognising the role of play in a child's wellbeing and the best interest of the child is vital, encourages the participation of the child in decisions that affect them. This refers to their education also, Article 28 of the UNCRC.

As play is a way in which children express themselves, develop life skills, learn, socialise, and participate in the world around them, it is vitally important we consider this when making decisions about their environments and the settings we are offering them. The UNCRC promotes the significance of play in early childhood, and it not only recognises the child's right to play but also highlights the broader implications of play for the child's wellbeing, development, and participation in society. The UNCRC is an important framework for advocating and promoting the rights of the child to engage in play in a variety of contexts, including education.

Summary

Montessori emphasised that play was more than a pastime; it is a child's meaningful engagement in purposeful activities that contribute to their overall growth and development. Montessori viewed play as the primary means through which children explore, experiment, and make sense of the world. Play is valued as essential work that facilitates physical, cognitive, social, and emotional development.

By honouring the child's natural inclination towards purposeful play, adults can support lifelong learners who approach challenges with curiosity, creativity, and resilience.

8 Freedom Within Limits

Box 8.1 Chapter Overview

By the end of this chapter, you will be able to do the following:

- Understand what is meant by freedom within limits.
- Appreciate the child's need for structure and boundaries.
- Understand the role of the adult and the prepared environment.
- Have clear understanding on how to foster freedom within limits in your environment.

What Is Freedom Within Limits?

The concept of "freedom within limits" is central to the Montessori philosophy and refers to the balance between giving children autonomy and providing them with the necessary structure and boundaries. Montessori observed that children have a natural inclination to explore and learn independently, and she believed in fostering this intrinsic motivation while guiding their behaviour within a prepared environment.

> Liberty is not to be free to do whatever one likes, but to be able to act without help.
>
> (Montessori, 1949, The Absorbent Mind)

With freedom comes responsibility, and there are three aspects we should embed in our environment to enable freedom within limits to succeed:

- Respect for oneself
- Respect for others
- Respect for the environment

Firstly, respect for oneself is demonstrated through working safely and productively with the environment and affords oneself the best opportunity for learning. Children are free to choose their activities, provided they have been shown how to use the activity.

Secondly, respect for others involves social skills and making good choices. Children have the choice to work independently or within a small group. However, they must be invited to work with another child and must respect the other child's work and not interfere. This builds on their place within their community.

Finally, respect for the environment relates to proper care for everything within the environment they are in. This includes the proper use of the materials, returning items to the shelves, and taking care of all living and nonliving things within the environment.

Understanding Freedom

Although often misunderstood, in the Montessori context, freedom does not imply a lack of structure or discipline. Instead, it refers to the liberty granted to children to choose their activities, explore their interests, and follow their natural curiosity. Montessori believed that children possess an innate drive to learn and explore their environment actively. Therefore, providing them with the freedom to engage in self-directed learning is crucial for nurturing their intrinsic motivation and fostering a love for learning.

> To let the child do as he likes when he has not yet developed any powers of control is to betray the idea of freedom.
> (Montessori, 1949, The Absorbent Mind)

The Role of Independence

Central to Montessori's concept of freedom is the development of independence in children. By allowing a child to make choices and take responsibility for their learning, we empower children to become self-reliant and confident individuals. Children develop life skills such as problem solving, time management, decision making, and critical thinking that are essential for their future learning.

Establishing Limits

Whilst freedom is valued, it is essential to recognise the importance of establishing limits. Limits serve as the scaffolding upon which children's freedom is built. Freedom cannot be given to the child all at once and without several considerations. Limits bring structure, and routine and provides the child with security and a sense of familiarity.

Promoting Responsibility

Through the expert modelling and guidance from the adults, the child will develop a sense of responsibility in the decisions they make. The child becomes an active participant in their learning and growth through the freedom of choice, and this establishes the sense of responsibility, as the child feels trusted to make those decisions.

Individual Guidance

Although there are limits for the whole classroom, we know that each child progresses at their own pace, and we afford the child the freedom to do this and offer individual guidance and support when needed. Each child needs time to build their independence and respond to the limits according to their own developmental needs.

Freedom Within Limits and the Child

Freedom within limits supports a child's holistic development and affords the child the autonomy to explore, learn, and grow within a structured (prepared) environment that provides necessary boundaries and guidelines.

- Autonomy and choice: Freedom of choice – a fundamental aspect of the Montessori approach is freedom of choice. Choice allows children to discover their own needs, interests, and abilities. It also encourages active engagement in their own learning.
- Self-expression and Creativity: Freedom of repetition – the uninterrupted work time affords the child the opportunity to repeat activities for as long as they wish to. This provides opportunities for the child to achieve success through practice and commitment. This also supports the development of problem solving skills.
- Responsibility and accountability: Freedom of time – uninterrupted work time is important for young children. A child should be free to work on an activity for as long as they like, as this supports children to not only learn at their own pace but also develop their focus and concentration skill.
- Social skills and collaboration: Freedom to collaborate – children are encouraged to communicate and discuss activities and scenarios with their peers. This communication develops their social skills and problem solving skills.
- Exploration and discovery: Freedom to move – children should be free to move around the room and move from one activity to the next. This freedom will promote purposeful work and exploration of their environment, which helps children discover their interests.
- Independence and self-reliance: Freedom to be true to self – children have the freedom to develop their independence in the security of an environment that has necessary limits. This freedom develops the children's autonomy and self-belief.

Personal Growth and Development for the Child

Freedom within limits supports the child's holistic development, encompassing cognitive, social, emotional, and physical domains. They can develop at their own pace, building upon their strengths and addressing areas for growth in a supportive and nurturing environment. Freedom within limits encourages a child to become a respectful member of their community, and through real life experiences, children learn to make choices that best serve their own needs and helps build independence and confidence.

At a very young age, children begin to demonstrate their desire to do things for themselves. Carefully and with intent, offer the child time and structures that allow independent self-care as much as possible. Examples of what this can look like in the environment are as follows:

- Preparation of snack
- Putting on their own coat/shoes
- Carrying their own work
- Independent in the toilet
- Washing hands

Freedom Within Limits and the Role of the Adult

The role of the adult should be viewed as a facilitator rather than instructor. The adult in the early years setting guides and supports the child in their learning journey, offering themselves as a mentor and resource. Through observation and knowledge of the child's needs and interests, the adult will be able to offer activities that provide opportunities for growth and development.

As the child grows, they require guidance and support to navigate their learning experiences. The adult will help when required or requested but also supporting the child to learn from errors and to persevere through challenges. It is also necessary to set clear expectations and boundaries for the child for them to know and understand what is expected of them and what the consequences are for the choices they make.

Examples of how the adult provides limits whilst offering freedom:

1. Preventing, redirecting, or stopping disruptive behaviours
2. Modelling expected behaviour
3. Grace and courtesy
4. Supporting children in difficult social situations
5. Giving choices
6. Preparing the environment

Freedom within limits can prove to be frustrating for the child and adult at times. We need to focus on the long-term benefits and remain consistent in what we offer. It will aid the children in their social skills, self-discipline, independence, and much more. With consistent modelling and guidance, the adult respects the child's journey whilst also reinforcing behaviours that support the peaceful environment.

Expectations to Support Freedom Within Limits

The first step to successfully offering freedom within limits is setting clear expectations ahead of time. Different environments will have different ways of addressing these expectations, such as classroom rules, community rules, community agreement, or our agreement. Ultimately, these are expectations that work for your community that the children are aware of. I encourage the involvement of children in deciding these expectations. Remain focused on the safety of self, others, and the environment and avoid using overly negative language when deciding these.

For example:

- Water stays in the jugs/cups/basins/sinks/etc. If it spills, we clean it up.
- Chairs are for sitting. We can climb outside (or indoors if there is equipment for climbing).
- We return activities to the shelves when we are finished. This allows our friends to have a turn.
- We talk respectfully to each other which means we do not shout across the room (that goes for the adults too).
- We are respectful, so do not interrupt others when they are working.

Box 8.2   Practice Activity

Consider the needs of your environment, and write a list of expectations you would like to embed. When you discuss expectations with the children, see if they have the same expectations as you.

Freedom Within Limits and the Prepared Environment

To be successful when offering the child freedom, you need to be intentional in the way you structure the physical environment for the child. Consideration needs to be given to the movement of the child, and whilst we want to and need to encourage movement, we do not want that movement to encourage behaviours that would be considered distracting or unsafe. As mentioned previously, it is our role as the adult to prepare the environment to offer success to the child. An example of this would mean strategically placing the shelves to block paths that would invite running in the environment.

Creating an optimal environment where children are free to grow and learn requires the environment to be organised, safe, inviting, and secure. An environment that welcomes the child to make choices and to progress through the carefully considered activities at their own pace offers freedom, but the limits come from the carefully curated selection of activities that are developmentally appropriate and, as much as possible, self-correcting.

With all the choice we afford children, ensuring we have only offered the child the activities we know they are ready for is the role of the adult and their observations. The activities put out for use by the child should be so beautiful and inviting that the child's interest will be heightened and want to use them. Think about the desired outcomes you want in the environment and create an environment that will allow children to achieve them with a level of independence, empowerment, and satisfaction.

Freedom Within Limits in Practice

- Freedom of time – as much as possible, allow the child the time they desire on their chosen activity without interruption.
- Freedom of choice – offer a wide range of activities for the child to freely choose from. The activities have been carefully prepared to meet the needs of the child and ignite their interests.
- Freedom to move – children have the freedom to move around their environment, developing their motor movements as they go. Children should also have the freedom to rest and observe if they are not disruptive to others.
- Freedom to make mistakes – children have the freedom to make mistakes, learn from them, and not be afraid of making them.

Communication is key for this approach to be effective within settings. Our communication with the children about limits should be clear and to the point. Recognising that the child may need time to respond to these limits, we need patience and consistency whilst they are processing their new limits. Use of language is important, as the overuse of the word "no" renders it ineffective and removes independence and autonomy from the child.

Box 8.3 Observation Case Study

This case study explores the interplay between autonomy and structure in an early year's environment. This environment is a traditional (non-Montessori) setting.

Michael is 4 years old and has been attending the setting for six months now. He is curious, energetic, and has an emerging sense of independence. The observation took place within the prepared environment that Michael spends much of his time in. The space is organised with age-appropriate activities and on easily accessible shelving.

> Observation: Michael enters the environment demonstrating excitement and eagerness to start his day. Michael chooses the art area to work in first and chooses a blank piece of paper and crayons. Michael makes marks on the paper using different colours to create his art piece.
>
> Michael moves to the creative area where he chooses a firefighter costume to wear. He looks at himself in the mirror and begins to act out as if he was putting out fires. Michael asks a friend to join him, and the two begin to role-play, creating several scenarios.
>
> Michael and his peer decide to have snack together. They continue to discuss their ability to put of fires and what great firemen they are! After snack, Michael starts to work with the blocks with a different friend. They collaborate to build a towering structure. They discuss solutions to problems they encounter, agree on a solution, and communicate how they will continue. Michael stops to check their surroundings, ensuring they have enough room to build their structure. Michael and his peer are offered guidance and support when their structure collapsed and they became upset.
>
> Conclusion: This case study highlights the balance between autonomy and structure in an early years setting. Through the lens of Michael's experiences, we observe how the adults create the prepared environment that promotes independence, creativity, and social interaction. By offering a variety of activities that Michael is free to choose and that spark his interest and exploration, Michael is learning in ways that reflect his unique interest and developmental needs. Michael is aware of the limits in the classroom having been there six months and demonstrates confidence in exploring freely.

Summary

The concept of freedom within limits is fundamental within a Montessori environment. It promotes independence, social and emotional development, self-discipline, problem solving skills, and critical and creative thinking in children. Freedom within limits encourages children to become respectful and active members of their communities (school, home, local, etc.). The real-life experiences offered to the child enables them to learn that freedom is making the choice that best serves themselves and others. Children learn to understand and respect the limits (rules), thus building independent and confident individuals.

> Let us leave the life free to develop within the limits of the good and let us observe this inner life developing. This is the whole of our mission.
> (Montessori, 1965b, Dr. Montessori's Own Handbook)

9 Hands-On Learning

> **Box 9.1 Chapter Overview**
>
> By the end of this chapter, you will be able to do the following:
>
> - Understand why Montessori advocated for children to be active in their learning and have hands-on experiences.
> - Appreciate the connection between the hand and the mind.
> - Reflect on your role in fostering independent learning and trusting the child's movements.
> - Understand how to prepare the environment to offer hands-on experiences for the child.
> - Reflect on the examples of activities to adapt to your own setting.

Introduction

Montessori believed if a child was able to use their hands to discover, their discoveries would become more meaningful to them. She believed that when children use their hands to learn, they experience their learning and become active participants in their learning.

> What the hand does, the mind remembers.
> (Montessori, 1949, The Absorbent Mind)

For children to learn about the world around them, they need tangible, physical experiences. Montessori believed in the value of active learning for the child because it connects them with the real world and believed that children learn best through active engagement with their environment, using their senses and manipulating tangible materials and activities.

Children should be encouraged to touch, manipulate, and explore the activities at their own pace. Montessori observed that children experienced joy when using their hands for learning. It was because of this that she designed the activities known as the "Montessori materials" that you see in Montessori environments around the world. These activities require the child to be actively using their hands to manipulate them. They intentionally foster self-discovery, exploration, and engagement.

Learning in early years should involve hands-on learning in all subject areas and throughout the environment. Montessori believed the child needs engagement with both their hands and their minds to grasp a concept.

Active Learning

It is well-known that children learn best when they are actively engaged with the learning process. Despite the awareness of this, early childhood education does not always look like this for the child, and many struggle to implement this into practice. Children are hard-wired to learn through movement, and Montessori emphasised the need for adults to offer direct experiences for the child, as she believed if a child uses their hands to discover the world around them, those experiences become more meaningful to the child.

Hands-On Learning and the Child

> Movement of the Hand is essential. Little children revealed that the development of the mind is stimulated by the movement of the hands. The hand is the instrument of the intelligence. The child needs to manipulate objects and to gain experience by touching and handling.
>
> (Montessori, 1946, The London Lectures)

Remembering that the early years environment is for the child, we should then provide them with the opportunity to be active within that environment and learn through hands-on experiences with the carefully prepared activities that meet their developmental needs.

Our early years child is not designed to sit still and passively go through the motions of learning. They want to get stuck in! We often talk about teaching children the skills they will need in the future, but Montessori believed hands-on experiences in the early years allows children to develop the skills they need now to be independent. The child is in control and has the freedom to explore the activities and discover concepts for themselves.

Box 9.2   Example Activity

The following example is the presentation of fabrics. It is a sensorial activity to develop the tactile sense and can be easily adapted to your setting with the use of different fabrics. Whilst the direct focus for this activity is the development of the tactile sense, the child is also developing their visual sense and deepening their focus and concentration.

Purpose: To develop the tactile sense – develops the child's ability to distinguish between different textures and sensations. Children will learn to classify textures based on their properties, such as smoothness or roughness.

Materials: A container with two of each of a variety of basic fabrics: silk, linen, cotton, wool, etc. Cut into identical shapes (square, circle), edges pinked. Each pair of fabric is a different colour and/or print. Ten pairs of fabrics minimum.

Presentation.

1. Inform the child that you both need to wash your hands before you begin this activity.
2. Invite the child to work with the fabrics and introduce the activity at the shelf.
3. Carry the container with the fabrics to the table.
4. Set it down and both sit down.
5. Once seated, from the container to the table, set out all the fabrics in random order.
6. Set the container aside.
7. Part A – matching with eyes open. Take one piece of fabric and feel it with both your hands. Use all of your fingers and thumb to feel the fabric thoroughly.
8. Set that fabric aside.
9. Tell the child that you are going to find the fabric that feels like the one you just set aside.
10. Feel one to two pieces of fabric that do not match the one you set aside and then take the one that does match.
11. Put the two pieces of fabric together that do match and set them aside.
12. Repeat steps 7–11 for three more pairs of fabric.
13. Invite the child to continue matching the remainder of the fabrics.
14. Once all the fabrics are matched, invite the child to check their work by separating each pair and feeling them again.
15. Part B – matching with eyes closed. Repeat part A exactly, except have your eyes closed during the matching and open them to check the work.
16. Invite the child to match the fabrics with their eyes closed.

Control of error: within the material.
Language: conversational.
Note: you could have another set of fabrics set aside that are all the same colour/pattern but are different textures that you could have the child work with after they have developed considerable facility with this activity.

86 Hands-On Learning

Figure 9.1 Fabrics Activity (Blindfolded)

The hands-on experiences help children develop a concrete understanding of concepts before moving to abstract as well as the following:

- Stimulate the child's mind
- Encourage exploration
- Inspire logical thought
- Developing independence

Learning through their senses allows children to have a fuller experience that enhances memory and creates lasting connections in the brain.

Hands-On Learning and the Adult

> Our care for the child should be governed, not by the desire to make him learn things, but by the endeavour to always keep burning within him that light which is called intelligence.
> (Montessori, 1965a, Spontaneous Activity in Education)

There are huge differences in how an adult learns and how a child learns. The child's brain is still developing as they absorb their environment during their early years. Understanding this difference is necessary for the adult to be able to prepare the child's environment to offer the hands-on experiences they need to develop.

- Stimulate the interest of the child – for them to be independent in the work they are choosing.
- Neutral-coloured environment to avoid overstimulation and promote the development of focus and concentration but also encourage sensorial exploration.
- Use your observation to prepare the activities that the child needs.
- Knowledge of child development is essential to meet the needs of the child.
- Self-reflection and self-awareness.

It is through the observations of the adult that you will notice what interests the child has and be able to adapt, create, and prepare activities accordingly. Preparation of the activities take into consideration the child's natural drive towards activity and their need to be doing.

Young children will learn by being shown, rather than being told what to do. Show the child. Take the time to present the activity to the child first and allow the child to touch and explore with their hands. When the child manipulates activities with their hands, they are also making connections to their brain, making use of the motoric memory. This offers a deeper learning experience for the child.

All aspects of the early years' environment should offer hands-on learning for the child. Activities such as washing a table shows care for the environment but also serves as preparation for writing. The hands-on learning fosters multiple objectives.

Box 9.3   Refection Activity

If you want to make one change straight away in your setting, start with the child's hands. Look at the activities you currently offer and consider the following:

- How many offers hands-on learning?
- How many afford the child the opportunity to explore independently?
- Which ones require the child to be active rather than passive?
- Can you add in more activities that offer hands-on learning?

Hands-On Learning and the Prepared Environment

> The environment must be rich in motives which lend interest to activity and invite the child to conduct his own experiences.
> (Montessori, 1967, The Absorbent Mind)

Montessori believed that children did not learn through rote memorization; instead, they require the hands-on experiences where they will learn by doing. Montessori emphasised that for this approach to be effective, it needs to go beyond busying the child's hand and aim to develop the child's self-motivation and make connections to the child's world.

The environment should direct the child towards self-development whilst developing concentration, focus, and confidence within their own abilities and development progress. The optimal prepared environment is based on the trilogy of the child, the adult, and the prepared environment working together and for each other. It is the interactions between the three that help children achieve cognitive, social, emotional, and physical attainments.

As discussed in Chapter 4, the early years child absorbs everything they are exposed to in their environment. A well-organised, child-focused, and purposefully prepared environment which captures organisation, beauty, simplicity, and order will influence the child's natural desire to have the sensorial experience of their own environment. The environment provides a calm and neutral space that encourages and supports learning.

The design of the environment needs to meet the goal of offering hands-on learning experiences for the child.

- Be attractive and inviting – display activities that are interesting, complete, and in working order and in order of difficulty
- Natural materials for optimal sensorial experiences
- Space for all areas of the curriculum to be available for use
- Child-size furniture
- Activities that can be self-correcting
- Freedom of movement
- Nonrestrictive

The environment needs to go beyond the physical aspects and ensure the child is free from unnecessary interruption and disruption. This comes back to the roles and responsibility of the adult.

Practical Life Activities and Hands-On Learning

> It is interesting to notice that where life is simple and natural and where the children participate in the adult's life, they are calm and happy
> (Montessori, 1946, The London Lectures)

The aim of practical life is to aid the child to independence in the physical and mental sense. The activities provide the child with what they need to be able to do for themselves. Examples of these activities are as follows:

- Pouring
- Scooping
- Transferring
- Sweeping
- Washing a table
- Opening and closing different containers
- Locks and keys
- Pasting

Figure 9.2 Practical Life Activity Examples

90 *Hands-On Learning*

Figure 9.3 Practical Life Activity Examples

Figure 9.4 Practical Life Activity Examples

Hands-On Learning 91

Figure 9.5 Practical Life Activity Examples

Figure 9.6 Practical Life Activity Examples

92 Hands-On Learning

Box 1.4 Example Activity

Lesson 1: This is a Presentation on Pouring Rice (Dry Pouring)

Purpose: 1. Control and coordination of movement. 2. Preparation for pouring water.
Age: 2+ years
Materials: tray, 2 identical jugs (one jug is ¾ full of rice)
Presentation: Invite the child to do the pouring rice activity.

1. Carry the tray to the table and set it down. Be sure the rice-filled jug is on the left side of the tray.
2. Both you and the child sit down with the child sitting to the left of you.

Figure 9.7 Pouring Activity

3. With the right hand, take the handle of the jug with rice. With the left hand, steady the base of the jug on the bottom left side with index and middle fingers.
4. Lift the jug and place the spout of the jug directly over the centre of the empty jug.
5. Tilt and pour out the rice until the jug is empty.
6. Set the now-empty jug down.
7. Rotate the tray in two movements 180 degrees counterclockwise so the tray is now in front of the child with the rice-filled jug on the right side of the tray.
8. Invite the child to do the activity.

Points of Interest: 1. Transferring the rice from one jug to the other (how fast to go). 2. The sound the rice makes when falling into the empty jug.

Notes: be sure to use appropriate rice that will not become sticky and clump together.

Lesson 2: This Is a Presentation for Unrolling and Rolling a Mat

Purpose: 1. Control and coordination of movement. 2. Preparation for all mat activities.

Age: 2+ years – prerequisite is carrying a mat.

Material: mat

Presentation:

1. Invite the child to come with you to where the mats are stored.
2. Ask the child to watch you.
3. Remove a mat from the mat storage and carry it to the desired spot.
4. While continuing to hold the mat, squat down to the floor. With both hands place the mat on the floor perpendicular to the body.
5. With the left hand, hold down the edge of the mat to the floor. With the right hand, begin unrolling the mat. When the right arm is completely outstretched, stop unrolling and kneel walk over to the remaining coiled part of the mat. Again, hold down the mat with the left hand and begin unrolling the mat.
6. Repeat step 5 until the mat is completely unrolled.
7. Ask the child to stand with you, and walk around the mat to make sure the mat is in a good place.
8. Go to the short end of the mat and kneel.
9. With full fist grip, begin rolling the mat up. Stop when arms are fully extended in front of you. Kneel walk closer to the mat, check that both coiled ends are even by tapping them with open hands, and then continue rolling.

94 *Hands-On Learning*

Figure 9.8 Rolling a Mat

> 10. When mat is completely rolled up, pick up with both hands and carry mat to the mat storage. Replace the mat to the mat storage.
> 11. Invite the child to choose a mat to unroll and roll.
>
> Points of Interest: 1. Placement of the mat on the floor. 2. Moving your body along with the mat as it is unrolled or rolled up.

Summary

Montessori recognised the pivotal role of tactile, experiential, and sensorial learning for the child. She emphasised the importance of hands-on exploration as a fundamental method for engaging children to be active in their own learning and to help foster a deep understanding. Montessori defines hands-on learning as involvement of all the senses.

Activities designed to be concrete and manipulative enable the child to explore concepts through tangible experiences. The hands-on experiences allow the child to make realistic connections between what they see, touch, hear, taste, and smell, also supporting their understanding of their world. Each activity offered to the child serves a specific purpose in fostering cognitive, motor, social-emotional, and physical development.

The practical life activities serve as the foundation in the environment offering benefits such as focus and concentration, exploration, motor development, social skills, independence, critical and creative thinking, problem solving, and emotional development. The adult's role is to observe the needs of the child to prepare an environment that is purposeful. Montessori highlighted the need for the acute awareness adults need to have on their own movements and refine their movements to model to the child.

10 Independence

> **Box 10.1 Chapter Overview**
>
> By the end of this chapter, you will be able to do the following:
>
> - Understand independence as a core principle in Montessori education.
> - Understand and respect the child's innate drive for independence and self-directed learning.
> - Be confident in your role to facilitate the growing independence of the young child.
> - Use your observations to reflect on the prepared environment as a support to the growing independence of the young child.

Introduction

It is in the child's natural drive to quest for independence. For a child to develop, they need to become independent. Independence and development are symbiotic. The word independent is defined as free from influence, guidance, or control of another, and it is the inner drive of the child to grow and move towards independence. It is important to recognise that independence is not a static state but a constant resolution of problems. Independence is an ongoing and organic process which will lead to ongoing benefits throughout life.

> Never help a child with a task at which he feels he can succeed.
> (Montessori, 1967, The Absorbent Mind)

One of the key principles of Montessori is to teach the child to be able to do things for themselves. We are there to provide opportunities for the child to engage in independent work. In Montessori environments, children are active agents in their own learning journey and set their own learning agendas.

Children are not required or expected to keep the same pace as others, and the activities and materials offered to the child are designed to encourage our young learners to assess their own learning progress and recognise challenges and errors. This supports the child to develop personal independence which leads to a sense of purpose and motivation.

An Aid to Life

Montessori believed that as humans, we must create a self or our personality as we mature. To aid the child to reach their full potential, we must try to understand their inner drive and offer an environment in which they can be supported to form their self. We are there to assist this development, not achieve it for the child.

The promotion of independence in the early years has profound implications for children's overall development.

- Self-Confidence and Self-Esteem
  When a child masters practical skills and begins to take on increasing responsibilities, they develop a sense of confidence and self-esteem. They learn to turn in their own abilities and capabilities, which supports their future resilience.
- Executive Functioning Skills
  Activities that are considered "independence-related," such as planning, organising, problem solving, and self-regulation, contribute to the development of executive functioning skills. These cognitive abilities are essential for lifelong learning, social competence, and emotional intelligence. The practical life activities lay the foundation for this skill development.
- Autonomy and Empowerment
  Promoting independence empowers children to become active participants in their own learning process. Children will develop a sense of agency, enabling them to begin to navigate the world with purpose and confidence.

Independence and the Child

For some, encouraging this level of independence goes against what society or culture tells us about raising children. We are told that children need us to do most tasks for them in their earlier years. However, children need us to trust them with the opportunity to try to do it themselves. Montessori believes that every child is born with a potential for independence. The child's drive for independence can often clash with the adult's expectation or need at that time. It can be hard to grasp the concept that whilst the child may not do the task as well as us at this stage, they will never learn unless they try.

> How does the child acquire independence? He acquires it using continuous activity. Independence is not static. It is a continuous conquest. And

98 *Independence*

using continuous work, one acquires not only freedom but strength and self-perfection.

(Montessori, 1967, The Absorbent Mind)

The early years child goes through that formative period constructing their personality and adapting themselves to their world. The interactions the child has with their environment build their self-confidence and independence. Children at this age are learning to function in their world, and independence is grown through the activities they are doing.

The child tells us they want to be independent and they are busy constructing themselves, and adults believe they are helping the child, but in fact, this unnecessary interruption is a hinderance to their development and growth. When children act and think for themselves, they are building their self-confidence, self-belief, and self-esteem.

Figure 10.1 Independence in Action

Independence 99

Figure 10.2 Independence in Action

Figure 10.3 Independence in Action

100 *Independence*

Figure 10.4 Independence in Action

Independence and the Adult

It is the role of the adult to provide the child with the environment and opportunities for them to work towards independence. Supporting the child to independence does not mean you are leaving them alone. Children will gain independence by practicing being independent but that requires the adult to trust the process.

Adults can do the following:

- Prepare the environment
- Observe
- Be intentional
- Make time
- Be a role model
- Ask questions

The role of the adult is to be the creator of opportunities for the child to practice being independent, rather than doing for the child. Young children want to feel they have control in their lives also, and one way to embed this is to ask questions and give choice to the child. Try and avoid the yes-no questions!

For example:

Instead of "Do you want fruit for your snack?" give the child the choice and ask, "Would you like a banana or an orange?"

You do need to be happy with the choices you are giving your child. This comes back to freedom within limits (see Chapter 8). When the child is young, limit the choices you are offering to begin with. It can be extremely overwhelming for the child to be faced with too many choices. By allowing the child to make simple, age-appropriate decisions not only supports their development of independence but can also be a deterrent to avoid frustration resulting in behavioural outbursts.

Independence and the Prepared Environment

It is part of our role as adults to try and remove the obstacles that hinder the child towards independence. Montessori referred to the ongoing struggle for everyone as the "unremitting toil." To foster a child's quest for independence, an early year's environment should have the following:

- Child-size furniture, materials, activities
- Freedom of movement
- Freedom of association
- Freedom of choice
- Freedom from the adult's opinion/judgment
- Freedom for repetition
- Activities that meet the needs of the child and provide an opportunity for self-correcting
- Freedom for the child to progress at their own pace

Montessori strongly believed it was important to help children build independence and through her observations recognised that practical life activities can assist the child with this. Practical life activities help the child learn basic skills such as pouring, buttoning, sweeping, etc. These skills help the child to take care of themselves, take care of others, and take care of the environment. Through these activities the child will gain independence whilst also developing their motor skills, focus, concentration, and hand-eye coordination.

> If teaching is to be effective with young children, it must assist them to advance on the way to independence. We must help them to walk without assistance, to run, to go up and down stairs, to pick up fallen objects, to dress and undress, to wash themselves, to express their needs in a way

that is clearly understood, and to attempt to satisfy their desires through their own efforts.

(Montessori, 1972b, The Discovery of the Child)

Take a moment to read the earlier quote again.

Box 10.2   Reflective Exercise

Write the tasks you ask of the child throughout the day/week and then check if you have given time to help the child become successfully independent with those tasks.

All too often, we expect the child to be able to do something (put socks on, wash hands, blow nose), but children are not born knowing how to do these tasks; they need to be shown how to do it.

Now consider what activities you can bring into your environment that are life skills.

Independence and Autonomous Development

Autonomy is an essential development in early childhood, and although often considered connected to independence, they both have different meaning.

To be autonomous: self-directed.

To be independent: not needing or not being influenced by others.

> We must clearly understand that when we give the child freedom and independence, we are giving freedom to a worker already braced for action, who cannot live without working and being active.
> (Montessori, 1967, The Absorbent Mind)

The prepared environment supports a child's autonomous development, especially within practical life activities. These activities allow the child to develop their ability to take care of their own needs independently. Through our observations, we will be prepared to guide the child in such a way that they will develop their independence to be able to direct their own learning. Montessori encouraged us to consider it a success when the child no longer needs us to support them in their tasks.

> The greatest sign of success for a teacher is to be able to say, "The children are now working as if I did not exist."
> (Montessori, 1964, The Absorbent Mind)

Independence and Uninterrupted Work Periods

There is a lot written on the idea of a three-hour uninterrupted work period within a Montessori early years environment for the 3- to 6-year-olds, but this is an argued expectation and also a challenge to be successful with for many settings. The recommendation is between one and three hours needs to be given to the child for the benefits of this uninterrupted work period to be effective. This will be dependent on the age of the children in your setting. Understanding and valuing the importance of an uninterrupted work period is the priority to be able to implement it to your setting for as long of a period that works for your setting, whilst serving its value and benefits for the child. The uninterrupted work period is fundamental to the Montessori approach for respect for the child's freedom to be independent in their choices and how long they wish to spend with each activity.

> The mind takes some time to develop interest, to be set in motion, to be get warmed up into a subject, to attain a state of profitable work. If at this time there is interruption, not only is a period of profitable work lost, but the interruption produces an unpleasant sensation which is identical to fatigue.
> (Montessori, 1989d, What You Should Know About Your Child)

Montessori observed children, even at a very young age, have the capacity of immense concentration when left to work without interruption. She noted that the adult becomes the barrier to the child's learning when they unnecessarily interrupt the child. For children to become independent, they need to be free from the barriers of interruptions.

To Implement Uninterrupted Work Period into Your Setting to Support Independence

Independence starts with the child hanging up their coat on arrival/changing to indoor shoes or whatever your setting does to acknowledge the transition from home. This will also include the greeting between the child and the adult and the child and their peers.

For some settings, this will work when the child arrives in the morning, but for others, it will be after the morning circle/group activity. The child chooses their first activity, and this is the start of their work period. Some children will be eager to begin whilst others will need a little more guidance to get started. When you are making this change in your setting, you need consistency, patience, and ensure you explain the change to the child. They cannot just be expected to work and be independent in the continuation of work if this has not been the norm to date.

Children in early years tend to choose to work alone but perhaps beside their friend. The activities within the early year's environment are mostly designed for individual work, again developing a sense of independence as well as self-achievement. The child chooses to work at a table or with a rug on the floor, and they use the activity in the way they have been showed. And when they choose to be finished, they return it to the shelf.

The adults in the environment need to ensure the environment is prepared for the child to be successfully independent and protect and respect their work period. Depending on how many adults are in the environment, each will play a role. The example here will work for three adults: one guide and two assistants. The assistants are responsible for keeping the environment neat and tidy, redirecting, or guiding the child when required but still respecting their independence. This allows the guide to focus of activity presentations and observations. During the work period, presentations tend to be non-group presentations, and the guide focuses on one-to-one with the child. The assistants protect the guide's work with the children during this period and intercept any potential interruptions.

If your assistants have been trained with how to observe the child, one may do this. Or if they have had training on activities such as sound games, they may take a small group of children that perhaps are struggling with choosing work and play a sound game with them. Or simply read a short book to a small group or supervise the children working outdoors (if you have an open-door policy between indoors and outdoors).

If an adult does need to speak to a child, it is done in a low tone and the child is interrupted the same way we have asked they interrupt the adult in our setting. It would be unreasonable to expect the child to remain focused for the extent of the work period. That is not what uninterrupted work period is meant to be. The child will take a break when they feel. This can be to observe a peer, have snack, sit, read, use the toilet, look out the window, or something other, but in line with Montessori principles, this is still the work of the child! They are independent in their choices during their work period.

Box 10.3 Case Study

Fostering Independence in Setting a Table

Within Montessori environments, children are active participants in the preparation of the environment for snack or lunch. Children are encouraged to develop life skills, including setting a table, as part of their self-care and community engagement.

To support the child in becoming independent in setting the table, the adult presents the lesson of how to set a table in the first instance. This can be done as a group activity or with individual children.

Steps of the activity:

Demonstration – the adult begins by demonstrating how to set a table step by step using child-sized utensils and tableware, purposefully slow with movements to emphasise the importance of precision and order.

Figure 10.5 Setting the Table

Hands-on practice – after the demonstration, the child/ren are invited to practice setting the table independently. The environment has a designated area with child-sized plates, cups, utensils, and napkins.

Support – if needed, the adult will offer support and guidance but will be careful not to "correct" the child. Using observation, the adult will be able to evaluate if the child/ren need another demonstration or a focus on one part of the activity at a later stage.

Peer collaboration – through practice and the social freedom in the environment, the children engage with each other, observing and learning from each other's actions.

Reflection/Reinforcement – after the child has had enough practice with this activity, the adult may choose to repeat the activity with language for the items used.

Through this hands-on experience, children are developing their confidence in practical tasks, fostering a sense of autonomy and self-reliance,

> and deepening their sense of achievement in their independent work. This activity also supports the development of fine motor skills, social skills, and responsibility.
>
> Practical life activities, such as setting a table, can naturally promote independence in young children. By empowering the child to engage in purposeful tasks, you are nurturing capable, confident, independent individuals who embrace responsibility.

Summary

Montessori believed that independence was a vital component of children's development, supporting them to become self-reliant, confident, and capable individuals. Independence refers to the child's ability to think, act, and make choices, being active participants and taking ownership of their learning and daily activities.

Our role in supporting the child to independence is to cultivate independence in all aspects of the child's life. We prepare an environment that encourages self-directed learning and foster autonomy. The child-sized furniture, activities, materials, and organisational space empower the child to engage independently. The offering of activities, such as the practical life activities, allow the child to contribute to their community in a meaningful way.

It is important to respect the child as an individual learner, one who will develop at their own pace and offer activities that empower each child. By utilising your observational skills, you are prepared to offer new activities and tasks when the child shows you their readiness. Prioritising the development of independence as a foundational skill empowers children to thrive.

11 Respect

> **Box 11.1 Chapter Overview**
>
> By the end of this chapter, you will be able to do the following:
>
> - Understand how respect for the child and the child's work is fundamental to fostering independence and self-motivation.
> - Value the importance of the relationship between the child and the adult in the environment.
> - Reflect on the language used when offering encouragement and how show respect to the child's efforts.
> - Recognise the importance of grace and courtesy activities fostering respect within the environment.

Introduction

Respect is incorporated in all aspects of Montessori pedagogy and, for me, is embedded in all work with children. Montessori highlighted the importance of affording children deep respect, not interrupting when they are concentrated, allowing them to discover and explore, staying away from the negativity of always pointing out mistakes, and of course, observing without judgment.

> Children are human beings to who respect is due, superior to us by reason if their innocence and of the greater possibilities of their future.
> (Montessori, 1964, The Absorbent Mind)

We live in a world where it is expected that children respect the adult, but Montessori believed that children should be respected too.

> The education of even a small child, therefore, does not aim at preparing him for school, but for life.
> (Montessori, 1972b, The Discovery of the Child)

DOI: 10.4324/9781003466970-12

108   *Respect*

In the Montessori world, you will often hear "follow the child" as a term used; it is the overarching focus of this book! This does not mean you follow the child around whilst they do as they please all day long! This means we remove our own assumptions about how things should be done and instead observe the child to see what the need and where their interest lies. We need to be reminded of the capabilities of the child. They can do so much more than we give credit for!

Society leads us to believe that we, the adults, are required to always engage with the child to be doing our jobs as parents, carers, or educators. However, Montessori believed that for us to "do our jobs," we need to step back and offer trust and freedom to the child.

> We must respect the child and he must understand that he is respected.
> He needs to be prepared for everything that is going to be done for him.
> (Montessori, 1946, The London Lectures)

When children feel respected, they are more likely to respect themselves and others. Here are some examples of how to show a child respect:

1. Actively listen
2. Acknowledge feelings
3. Show trust
4. Give choices
5. Respect boundaries
6. Show empathy
7. Acknowledge effort
8. Encourage independence
9. Show love
10. Be a role model

Respect is not merely a superficial gesture but a fundamental attitude that should guide every interaction between the adult and the child. Montessori emphasised the need to view children as individuals with their own unique capabilities, interests, and developmental needs, thus rendering us to afford respect to them for they hold more potential than we do.

Respect and the Child

There is a great need to respect the child as an autonomous person to support their individuality and capabilities for their future. As adults, it is often our inclination to protect the child, and I am sure you agree this is necessary, but our intentions may at times get in the way of the child's individual journey.

We must learn to trust the child is capable of doing things for themselves. Recognition is needed that children are at different stages of development and will learn in different ways. An environment that understands this will value the one-to-one opportunities between the adult and child, meaning different learning needs can be accommodated.

Children are seen as active participants in their own learning rather than passive recipients of knowledge. Montessori recognised that every child is unique with their own strengths, and by embracing the individuality of each child, we will recognise that diversity enriches the learning environment, creating inclusivity where every child feels valued and respected.

Respect and the Adult

You cannot expect the child to show or understand respect if you don't show them how. Montessori spoke intensely about the need for respect for the child but also highlighted that the child in return will show respect to self, others, and their environment.

> As a rule, we do not respect children. We try to force them to follow us without regard to their special needs. We are overbearing with them, and above all, rude; and then we expect them to be submissive and well-behaved, knowing all the time how strong their instinct of imitation and how touching their faith in and admiration of us. They will imitate us in any case. Let us treat them, therefore, with all the kindness which we would wish to help develop in them.
> (Montessori, 1965b, Dr. Montessori's Own Handbook)

Modelling respect to the child will become part of the environment.

- Actively listen when the child speaks to you – remain attentive. The child's words are important and deserve your attention and time. You are showing respect to the child as you listen and connect with the child through their words.
- Value the child's emotions. The child may not be able to articulate their emotions, but you can offer them a safe and secure space to explore their feelings and learn how to express their emotions effectively.
- Be purposeful with your language, and use kind and considerate words. Use the language you wish for the children to use. "Please" and "thank you" are simple examples of being respectful.
- Treat others with kindness. Show the child how you greet others with respect and kindness and how your treatment of others is still filled with kindness when they are not present.

Respect and the Prepared Environment

Building a respectful community within your environment takes conscious and purposeful dedication from the adult. Every individual is afforded respect and made to feel welcome and safe within the prepared environment.

- Value others' voice
- Use kind and considerate language
- Be mindful of others' space (personal and physical)

Montessori believed that children were the answer to achieve a more peaceful world, and respecting the child was paramount within her approach. Prioritise the child's voice. Encourage their thoughts, choices, and actions to shape the prepared environment – their community. Respect is shown to all through active listening, observing, and responding to the needs of the child.

Having classroom management is key here, but modelling the expectations of the environment is the role of the adult. If you do not want children to shout across the room to talk to a friend, you must not shout across the room. By walking over to talk quietly to someone, you are modelling how to respect others who are working and respect the peace within the environment.

Respect the Child's Work

Montessori believed that everything the child does is their work.

> Children live in a world of their own interests, and the work they do there must be respected, for although many activities of children may seem pointless to grown-ups, nature is using them for her own ends. She is building mind and character as well as bone and muscle.
> (Montessori, 1989b, The Child, Society and The World)

Adults can become frustrated when a child is insisting on doing the task themselves or when they want the same activity to work with repeatedly or the same book read repeatedly. We may even have the urge to rush them along or encourage them to choose something different, but the child knows what they need to develop more than we, the adults, do.

Respecting the work of the child show trust and belief in the child.

> Respect all the reasonable forms of activity in which the child engages and try to understand them.
> (Montessori, 1989, The Child and The Family)

Praise Effectively

There is a misconception that we do not praise in Montessori. This is not true! We are just effective and purposeful in how we offer praise to the child. Montessori believed that the sensitive periods (see Chapter 5) provide the child with the internal urge and reinforcement more than any praise or reward can do. Montessori works without the use of rewards and punishments.

Repeatedly telling a child that everything they do is wonderful or they are the best at everything can create a fear of failure within a child. Montessori had the utmost respect for the child's work and regarded it so highly that she believed this trust and respect for their work was praise enough.

However, praise related to the effort of the child's task is more effective if it is specific. Sometimes a simple "you finished your work" or "you did that all by yourself" is all that is required to acknowledge the effort of the child. Remember, we are encouraging independence! Learning to offer encouragement over praise is empowering to the child to make judgment of their own work or behaviour. They become reflective.

> What we need is a world full of miracles, like the miracle of seeing the young child seeking work and independence and manifesting a wealth of enthusiasm and love.
> (Montessori, 1992a, Education and Peace)

Changing how you do this can be challenge at first. It has become the natural response to say "good job" or "well done" after a child has done something. Become conscious of your responses and try something like "you worked hard to finish that work" or "look, you put everything away so carefully." Focus on the effort with sincerity.

Grace and Courtesy

> A child who becomes a master of his actions through repeated exercises of grace and courtesy, and who has been encouraged by the pleasant and interesting activities in which he has been engaged, is a child filled with health and joy and remarkable for his calmness and discipline.
> (Montessori, 1972b, The Discovery of the Child)

Grace and courtesy lessons are lessons of isolated behaviours the adults wish to model for the child. They involve everyday tasks, and Montessori highlights the need to support the child in their social forms. These lessons help children socialise in a respectful way and be participants in the community in respectful ways.

Aside from modelling these social norms, the adult offers lessons for the child to help them become independent. Here are a few examples of grace and courtesy lessons, but they are not limited to these:

- How to greet one another
- How to welcome
- How to say goodbye
- How to interrupt
- How to participate in a group activity
- How to invite yourself to a group
- How to listen in a conversation

- How to resolve conflict
- How to walk indoors
- How to get someone's attention without interrupting
- How to hold a door for someone
- How to take turns
- How to pass someone respectfully
- How to wash hands before eating
- How to blow your nose (see example later)
- How to check on someone's wellbeing (Are you ok?)
- How to carry a chair
- How to sit at a table
- How to tuck in a chair
- How to observe
- How to invite a friend to work with you

The list can go on and is culturally adaptable as well as adaptable to meet different age groups. Grace and courtesy lessons can be in the moment when you see it necessary and planned in advance to offer a group lesson if you see the environment needs it.

Developing grace and courtesy nurtures the child discovery of self-discipline and self-control. This requires patience and practice both from the adult and the child. The adult models the desired behaviour of the child. Lead by example.

Grace can be considered as self-awareness and the ability to conduct yourself in a respectful and acceptable way. Courtesy can be considered how we respect and value others. Montessori viewed grace and courtesy as a vital aspect for social development.

Box 11.2 Case Study

Garden City Montessori School caters for children 2 to 6 years of age, and respect for the child permeates every aspect of the learning environment. Henry joins the classroom with a strong interest in art. He is quiet, can become overwhelmed in group situations, and often struggles with transitions.

The adult embodies the principles of respect for Henry in its practice (and all children)

1. Observation – Henry's guide begins by observing Henry's behaviours, interests, and needs. They take note of Henry's interest for art and his challenges with transitions and group activities. It is through these observations that the guide gains insights into Henry's individuality and able to tailor their approach accordingly.

2. Individualised learning environment – Garden City Montessori values the child's individual learning journey and unique needs and interests. Henry's guide sets up the art area within the environment with a variety of materials for Henry to explore. Henry is encouraged to spend time exploring the art activities whenever he feels like it, when he is overwhelmed, or when he needs a break from the group activities. This space is designed to provide Henry with a sense of comfort and security.
3. Freedom of choice – Montessori emphasises the importance of allowing children to make choices about their learning experiences. Henry is given the freedom to choose the art materials and other materials or projects that interest him. Henry's autonomy is respected and valued, as he is afforded the freedom to explore at his own pace, be this art techniques and mediums or other. Henry is empowered to be creative.
4. Guidance and support – when needed, Henry is given gentle guidance and support, and when Henry shows he is struggling with transitions or social interactions, reassurance and assistance is given. By acknowledging Henry's feeling and offering support without judgment, a safe and nurturing environment is created where Henry feels valued and respected.

Through the implementation of respectful practices, Henry flourishes at the Garden City Montessori early years setting. He develops confidence in his own abilities, builds resilience in navigating social interactions, and experiences a sense of belonging within the learning community. Henry's individuality is respected, fostering holistic growth and development.

This case study demonstrates how being respectful of the child recognises and honours a child's individual journey and acknowledges their interests and needs. The observational practice is necessary for the adult to understand the child needs at that time, and throughout the practices of the adult with Henry, he is also absorbing how to be respectful and accepting of others.

Box 11.3   Grace and Courtesy Lesson on Blowing Your Nose

But no one really teaches them how they should blow their noses. When I tried to do so, they indicated that I had not only treated them with justice but had enabled them to get a new standing in society. I have come to appreciate the fact that children have a deep sense of personal dignity.

(Montessori, 1972a, The Secret of Childhood)

Purpose: 1. Control and coordination of movement. 2. Care of self and others. 3. Basic hygiene.
Age: 2+ years
Materials: box of tissues and mirror
Presentation:

1. Invite the child to the mirror to blow the nose.
2. Stand with the child in front of the mirror.
3. Take one tissue, and place it into the left hand.
4. Poke a pocket into the tissue, and place over the nose using one hand.
5. Blow the nose, clearing both nostrils.
6. Fold the tissue in half to contain any mucus.
7. With two hands, clean the nostril area with the folded issue, looking into the mirror.
8. Throw the tissue in the rubbish bin.
9. Wash your hands.
10. Invite the child to blow their nose.

Points of Interest: 1. Taking one tissue. 2. Blowing out and not in. 3. Containing all the mucus in the tissue. 4. Washing the hands afterwards.
Notes: do this exercise regardless of whether the child needs to blow their nose or not. Always aim to do this exercise in front of the mirror.

Figure 11.1 Blowing Nose Station

Summary

Respect is an invaluable character trait that when learning and practiced from early childhood will stay throughout the child's future years. Montessori believed that respect was of paramount importance, as it forms the foundation for all meaningful human interactions and learning experiences. It is through respect that individuals acknowledge each other's dignity, autonomy, and worth, fostering an environment conductive to growth, collaboration, and empathy.

Montessori valued respect for fostering harmonious relationships but equally for nurturing the development of self-discipline, responsibility, and a sense of belonging within a community. Montessori advocated for respect to be afforded to the child, as it serves as a guiding principle that cultivates a culture of kindness, understanding, and mutual support and guidance essential for society.

12 Language

> **Box 12.1 Chapter Overview**
>
> By the end of this chapter, you will be able to do the following:
>
> - Understand the importance of spoken language in developing skills to read and write.
> - Explore the child's introduction to writing and reading.
> - Understand the role the prepared environment has in supporting the child's language development.
> - Consider your role in the preparation of the environment and activities to foster a language-rich environment.

Introduction

Language is all around us, and Montessori stressed that children have a thirst for language and communication. Children's language development begins long before they enter the classroom. Studies show that children begin developing language even before birth. Children hear and internalise language from a wide variety of sources each day. Montessori believed that children could learn language simply by living around others who were using language. She identified that children are in the sensitive period for language from before birth to about 6 years of age. As if by magic, children not only internalise the language they are being exposed to but they also begin to sort out grammatical structure and even learn a second language during this time.

> A child can only acquire the words he hears spoken around him. This is not teaching but absorption. The child is, by nature, hungry for words; he loves strange, long words like names of dinosaurs and constellations. He takes all these words without understanding their meaning, as his mind is still taking language in by a process of unconscious absorption.
> (Montessori, 1946, The London Lectures)

We use language in many ways: via verbal communication, body language, sign language, music, writing, reading, and dance. Man is superior because our language separates us from animals of the world. Whilst animals also have ways of communicating, it is the written word that is completely unique to humans. In every day, hour, minute, or even second, the human mind is having thoughts that are processed in terms of language. We cannot think about language without using language in our minds to think about it.

> Language is an instrument of collective thought.
> (Montessori, 1964, The Absorbent Mind)

Language, the Absorbent Mind, and the Sensitive Periods

> The child must be born without any language at all so that he can take in the language of his environment. This is the work of the first two years of life – to take in a complete language. Whether a child is born in London, or Peking, or Paris, he must acquire the language that is around him.
> (Montessori, 1946, The London Lectures)

As with other areas of the environment, the language area also addresses the child's sensitive periods, allowing the absorbent mind to continue its journey to finish itself. The following are all the sensitive periods and how your language area within your environment can support them:

- The sensitive period for language – your entire environment should provide the child with keys to the world of written and verbal language, but a specific language area will focus on this more. The activities within this area should enhance vocabulary, increase the child's powers of expression, and lead them ultimately to the written word.
- The sensitive period for movement – many language activities require a great deal of motor movement. For example, the verb game can have the child perform many actions as they read them! Imagine how much more exciting it is to hop when you have just read the word for the first time. Once the child performs this activity, the idea that the verb is an action word will be brought into the absorbent mind and never forgotten.
- The sensitive period for order – all the language activities should have an order to them that is consistent because the child is moving towards reading and writing. Activities set up left to right (if that is how you read and write), the child will observe the adult writing from left to right, and using activities this way will solidify the child's sense of order.
- The sensitive period for refinement of sensorial exploration – within your language area, the child begins to write for themselves, which is something

he has unconsciously been preparing for through the other areas of the environment. Once the child puts his hand to chalkboard or paper, he will begin the process of refining his use of the writing instruments he is provided.

Language and the Child

Before the child is even linguistic, the language that surrounds them is already becoming fixed in the child's mind. Whatever the child hears will have an impact on how they perceive the world and themselves. Remember, the child is in their absorbent mind stage, so it is important to have awareness of their sensitivity to language at this stage to be able to assist the development of the whole personality of the child. This development of the personality is what is important, as this will allow the child to come forward in the world with grace and confidence.

Montessori recognised that children have a thirst for language and communication, and we must foster this foundation in spoken language. Adults can support and facilitate the acquisition of spoken language but cannot directly teach it. Grounded in all aspects of Montessori, hands-on activities serve the child best as they explore language and literacy. The goal is creating confident, independent, and creative readers and writers, fostering a love of reading and writing in the child.

Children in early years are in a sensitive period for language, meaning it is the perfect time to offer a language-rich environment when the child is naturally receptive to learning language and can acquire new vocabulary and grammar rules with ease. Writing and reading are two layers of the child's development that are based on the spoken word the child already has. Writing requires both physical and mental capacity that comes from within; we think of what we want to say and then we write it. Writing is a silent form of communication.

There are many physical abilities requires for writing, such as control and coordination of movement and lightness of touch. Montessori also emphasised the importance of preparation of the child's hand for writing. The practical life activities provide opportunities for the child to develop their fine motor skills, hand-eye coordination, and focus and concentration. These activities strengthen the child's muscles in their hand and fingers, which leads to their ability to hold a pencil and write.

> Thus we would use a kind of gymnastics to prepare the mechanisms of the hand. This preparation can be compared, in view of its goal, to the other, intellectual preparation for writing, achieved by means of the moveable alphabet. The mind and the hand are prepared separately for the conquest of written language and follow different roads to the same goal.
>
> (Montessori, 1989e, The Formation of Man)

Montessori identified that children who have had sufficient indirect preparation (practical life activities) will spontaneously write before they read. In most cases, children will write first and then, within approximately six months, will begin to read as well.

Language and the Adult – Preparation of Self

Montessori emphasised the real preparation for teaching is always the study of oneself. The adult must know themselves well so as not to impart to the child the weakness we all carry within ourselves. In relation to language, our pronunciation and vocabulary is crucial because what the child hears is the basis for their entire footing in language. Based on this, the adult should be able to use appropriate, varied, clear language around the child to enhance the child's development of language.

It is important for the adult to be knowledgeable regarding the development of language in the early year's child. When the adult knows the language development in the 0–3 child, they will be aware of where the child needs to go in the following stage of development. The 0–3 child teaches themselves the spoken language by absorbing whatever language is around them during this period. In many ways, the child at this level goes through the entire evolution of man, and therefore, it is valuable for the adult to also have a firm knowledge of the history of language itself.

We are aware that expression and communication are important; we converse with each other all the time. The child senses the significance of this communication and, in turn, learns to communicate and become part of society in this manner. As the child observes the adults around him speak back and forth to each other, he realises that this type of interaction is necessary to become a complete member of their community environment. Montessori believed if we are unable to communicate with others, we are isolated from society.

Language and the Prepared Environment

The child's environment is vital if he is to be successful in his endeavours to communicate with others. There are two components to the child's environment that the adult should consider:

1. Tangible environment – this is everything the child can see, hear, and touch. All the language for the activities in the environment and everything that is heard is important to the child's language development. Therefore, the activities must be correct and have proper spelling, grammar, punctuation, and accurate information. The library area or book corner within the environment should have carefully selected books for the child: picture books with and without text, scientific books, atlases, real-life stories, poetry, realistic books. The adult's own language should be precise, correct, and have a varied vocabulary. The adult should be ready to listen to the child when they speak, giving them full attention, face to face and with proper eye contact.

2. Intangible environment – these are the things that cannot be seen or heard, but they can be felt by the children in your environment. The intangibles of the environment can make the space a spectacular learning environment or can hinder the child's learning, depending on what the child absorbs. The adult needs to have strong faith and conviction that language is an important human expression that should be given a certain amount of reverence. The adult in the environment should have knowledge of the child's sensitive periods and how language is affected by these periods. Language has connections to all sensitive periods.

The language activities within the environment should build on what the child has already developed in the spoken word. This environment should provide highly enriched language and the possibilities for further experience and exploration of language. Activities should offer opportunities for the child to bring on his own development, and Montessori believed that if the child could absorb the spoken word in two years' time, then they would also be able to teach themselves to read and write spontaneously if they were provided the keys to the world of the written word.

> This is why we must offer the child the help he needs and be at his service so that he does not have to walk alone.
> (Montessori, 1964, The Absorbent Mind)

Figure 12.1 Language in the Prepared Environment

Language 121

Figure 12.2 Language in the Prepared Environment

Figure 12.3 Language in the Prepared Environment

122 *Language*

Figure 12.4 Language in the Prepared Environment

Figure 12.5 Language in the Prepared Environment

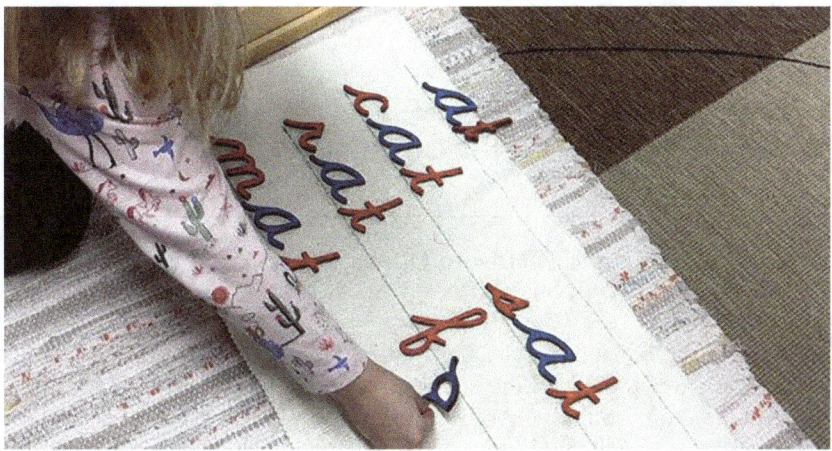

Figure 12.6 Language in the Prepared Environment

A language-rich environment for the child allows for adaptation to enable the child to develop the confidence to express themselves. It is a welcoming environment that is safe and secure. When preparing the environment, the adult must have the language needs of the child in mind to enhance the language the child already has so he can become adept at expressing himself well. Over time with the purposeful activities and purposeful intent of the adult, the child will become consciously aware of language, and the adult provides the keys to reading and writing.

Three Period Lesson

The three-period lesson comes from Edouard Seguin (1812–1880), a physician and educator who worked with children with disabilities, using this method to support the children in making a connection between an object and its corresponding object.

The three-period lesson is a fundamental technique used in Montessori classrooms around the world to engage the child with new concepts and vocabulary in a structured and effective manner. It engages children actively in the learning process, homing in on their natural curiosity, and promotes meaningful understanding and comprehension of information.

To summarise, it is a lesson in three parts. Typically, in Montessori environments, it is mostly used in the language area of the environment, but it can easily be used to teach other learning areas, such as numbers, colours, etc.

Offering the child, the opportunity to move from an introductory level of understanding to mastery at a pace that meets their needs allows the child to build confidence and knowledge of concepts. Unlike traditional lessons, there is no time frame for when each period begins or ends, but we do not move on to the next period until we know the child is ready.

The three-period lesson includes the following:

1. Introduction (This is)
2. Association/Recognition (Show me)
3. Recall/Mastery (What is this?)

Box 12.2   Example of How to Offer a Three-Period Lesson. I Am Using Shapes

Material: three shapes (circle, square, triangle)
Note: A three-period lesson can be used with children from about 18 months, but you are choosing items the child has been exposed to, and this is used to isolate the vocabulary to familiar items/objects. If the child is still learning how to talk, do not proceed to the third period.

The First Period – Introduction

- Point to the first item (square) and say, "Square."
- Clearly and slowly, repeat the name several times, "This is a square. Can you say square?"
- The child will repeat the word.
- Continue with the second and third shapes (circle and triangle).
- Once all three shapes have been named, review them, pointing at each one and saying the name.

If the child has been successful in this period, you move on.

The Second Period – Association/Recognition. This period is a much longer process than the first period. Take your time here, and don't rush the process.

- Rearrange the shapes in front of the child.
- Ask the child to show you a specific shape. "Show me the square."
- Ask the child to carry out different tasks. "Can you move the square to here?" Pointing to where you want the child to move it to. "Can you place the square in my hand?" etc.
- Repeat this with the other shapes, changing the tasks if you wish.
- Ask the child to close their eyes and move the shapes around and repeat the process.

Only if the child was successful in this period should you move on. If not, stop here and return for the third period at a later stage when the child has gained more confidence with the second period.

The Third Period – Recall/Mastery. This is the period where you are checking the child's knowledge. You will be confident the child will be successful here before proceeding.

- Place the three shapes in front of the child.
- Point to the first shape to the far left and ask the child, "What is this?"
- Repeat with the second and third shapes.

If the child is unsuccessful here, repeat the names to the child and end the activity to return when the child has worked more with the first and second period.

Box 12.3   Example Activity: Sound Games

Purpose: to isolate the sounds in words
Age: approximately 3 years
Materials: farm animals, clothing
Note:

1. It is important to do these as often as possible.
2. Sound games are done with phonetic and grapheme sounds.
3. The sounds you choose can be anywhere in the word to give the impression that sounds are all throughout the word.
4. Try to isolate the sound you are making.

The following are five examples of sound games, but there are many, many more.

Presentation 1 – Clothing

1. This can be done anytime and anywhere with any child.
2. Determine what the child is wearing by asking them to tell you.
3. Ask them for words with certain sounds pertaining to their clothing, e.g., Are you wearing something that has sound /p/ in it?
4. Repeat several times, with several different sounds.

Presentation 2 – Activities in the environment

1. This can be done at any time in the environment with any child.
2. Name some of the activities on the shelf with the child.
3. Ask the child to find something amongst the activities that has sound, for example, /a/.
4. Repeat several times, with several different sounds.

> **Presentation 3** – Farm animals
>
> 1. Invite between one and three children to work with you.
> 2. Bring the basket of farm animals to the table or on a rug on the floor.
> 3. Ask each child for an animal that has sound . . . in it.
> 4. Repeat several times, with several different sounds.
>
> **Presentation 4** – Materials within an activity
>
> 1. Invite a child to work with you.
> 2. Carry an activity that the child is familiar with to a table or on the floor (depending on activity).
> 3. Layout the activity with the child, giving the language for each material within the activity.
> 4. Return items to the basket/container/tray via a sound game by asking the child to put away an item that has a particular sound in it ("Can you please put away the item that has sound /b/ in it?").
> 5. Continue until all items are put away.
>
> **Presentation 5** – In the cloakroom
>
> 1. This can be done with all the children in the cloakroom or with one child.
> 2. Ask them to put on the item that has sound . . . in it.
> 3. Repeat until the children are all dressed to go outside or at least have several items on!

Introduction to Writing

Writing and reading are two layers of the child's development that are based on the spoken word the child already has. Writing requires both physical and mental capacity that comes from within; we think of what we want to say and then we write it. Writing is a thought that is put on paper broken down into a variety of sounds and symbols.

There are many physical abilities required for writing: control and coordination of movement, lightness of touch, ability to form the shapes of the letters with their hand and adapt their hand to the available space. Mentally, the child must also have the ability to think or have thoughts to express the words for the thought, ability to visualise the letters that make up the word, ability to think about the sounds for those letters, and ability to break down a word and then put it together to express it. That's a lot, isn't it?

Montessori stated that we must help the child prepare their abilities first and believed with the right activities and the prepared environment, the child will spontaneously come to writing. The indirect preparation, such as the activities in practical life, sound games, stories, and singing are all supporting the child's mind and, in some ways, their hand for writing. Montessori observed that if the child has had sufficient indirect preparation, they will spontaneously write before they read.

Montessori encouraged us to focus on the indirect preparation for writing and later focus on the beautifying of that writing. Encouraging children to use chalkboards long before the child writes on paper enables the child to practice without the permanence of writing on paper. The chalkboard helps the child build confidence to repeatedly practice their writing without the evidence of mistakes.

Introduction to Reading

Montessori noticed that it was approximately six months between writing and reading for most children. She also indicated that the prereading period is as critically important as the prewriting period. If we are aiming for a healthy development in the child, then the spoken language is the whole foundation for reading and writing and should be revered.

A Montessori environment will have an array of activities that prepare the child for reading, such as classified cards, storytelling, enrichment of vocabulary, and songs and poems, and the child will develop their ability to bring their spoken language into consciousness. Reading is also an explosion of awareness for the child because he becomes aware of the idea that what is being read are other people's thoughts. Writing comes first because it is a simpler analysis of words than reading. In writing, the child can put down their own thoughts; in reading, the child sees someone else's words, dissects them by sound, and then assembles the meaning inside their head. Reading is interpretive, and the child is required to take in the sounds and synthesise them.

The child will begin by reading words, then phrases, and then sentences. As with spoken language where children need to be exposed to people speaking, children need to be exposed to people reading to support them on their journey to reading independently. There is a technical ability and an interpretive ability to reading. Looking at the word and reading it is the technical part, but to understand or interpret the meaning of the words is a different skill completely. For the child to be a total reader, they must possess both the technical and interpretive abilities. We need to make sure that the child becomes consciously aware of the language they use.

Instil a Love of Reading

Instilling a love of reading in a child is the greatest gift one can give to another human being. Once a person loves to read, there are no limits to what that person can do in their lifetime. Read often and read a variety of texts to the children. Expose the children to the beauty and magic of books from an early age to form a natural part of their lives.

Remember, the young child is in the absorbent mind; they are looking to others to foster this love of reading so when we approach reading as if it is a chore, we are exposing the child to negative messages about reading. Here are a few suggestions to get you started:

1. Create an inviting space for reading – comfortable and accessible for the child.
2. Have a variety of books available for the child to choose from.
3. Don't be afraid of picture books!
4. Read every day to the children, at least once.
5. Tell stories to the children.
6. Make books with the children (about the child, the stories they make up, a trip, etc.).
7. Show the children how to respectfully handle books.
8. Model reading for your own enjoyment.
9. Create activities based on books.
10. Get excited to share books with the children.

Summary

Montessori recognised that children hear and internalise language from a wide variety of sources daily in their lives, and during their absorbent mind phase, this language is naturally forming part of their development. They become native speakers through absorption of language, naturally. Montessori emphasised the important role adults play in preparing a language-rich environment for the child.

Understanding what the child needs to go through to develop fully in language can remind us to slow down and not rush this process. Every child learns at their own pace and should not be restricted to meet the same goals as their peers. Montessori highlighted that spoken language forms the foundation for writing and reading, and adults need to be conscious of the language they are exposing children to.

The practical life activities indirectly support the children with writing and reading. These activities develop the hand for writing and the focus and concentration, hand-eye coordination, and sequencing (left to right and top to bottom) to support both reading and writing.

13 Mathematics

> **Box 13.1 Chapter Overview**
>
> By the end of this chapter, you will be able to do the following:
>
> - Understand Montessori's approach to early mathematics.
> - Recognise how to identify the child's sensitive period for mathematics.
> - Understand the importance of offering concrete activities before moving to abstract.
> - Appreciate the role you play in embedding a love of mathematics and preparing an environment to offer hands-on opportunities in mathematics.

Introduction

Mathematics is a universal language that gives humanity a way of dissecting patterns and regularities in the universe. Mathematics is all around us, and if we consider the everyday life of a young child, they are absorbing math daily, i.e., "Would you like MORE or LESS water?" or sorting, measuring, and quantity. I am sure you can think of many more examples of daily interactions with children that can stem back to math. Math is inherently abstract, and children absorb their foundations of math through their environment.

The word mathematics comes from the Greek word "mathencian," meaning "inclined to learn" which aligns with how Montessori observed the child as naturally curious and wanting to learn. Montessori believed the mathematical mind can be supported for children from an early age to stimulate their mathematical intelligence. Montessori believed that children are naturally inclined to create order, organise, observe relationships, and recognise patterns. Within a purposeful prepared environment, with activities that support this, children can develop their ability to reason and to calculate.

There are two aspects to mathematics, informal and formal. The informal mathematics is what we do in our everyday lives without thinking about it in

DOI: 10.4324/9781003466970-14

a mathematical way, i.e., how much time we have to leave the house! Aside from the calculations we do each day, as humans, we perform mathematically just by living; our bodies are precise mathematical machines. The human body functions a certain number of heart beats per minute, burns a certain number of calories per activity, takes a certain number of breaths per minute, and maintains a certain level of blood pressure per square inch of matter. We carry out mathematics by living and breathing every day!

Formal mathematics is abstracted by the human mind. Mathematics gives names, symbols, and equations to these abstractions. Many people have lived their lives working out equations and explanations for new abstractions/theories with the language of mathematics. Mathematics is more part of our lives than most people realise, and by exposing children to this world of symbols, we bring them further into our world in a profound and important way.

Montessori also emphasised the importance of offering the child the concrete before the abstract in all aspects in their learning, and math is no different. Concepts such as numeration, place value, fractions, and the basic operations of addition, subtraction, multiplication, and division can be offered in early years.

Pattern of Presentation in Mathematics

Throughout the mathematics area, there are certain patterns of presentation that assist the child's mathematical mind in classifying and solidifying the concepts presented. The child is first presented with the concrete before moving to the symbols and then moving to the combination of the concrete and the symbol together. In a Montessori environment, this would be the introduction to the number rods first, then the sandpaper numerals, and finally, the combination of both. Much like other areas within the early year's environment, the mathematics area should offer the child the whole and then move to the parts; for example, present the child with the numbers 1–9 and 0 first, which constitutes all the numbers in the whole number systems.

Consistency of language used to identify the concrete materials is also important. Language itself is important to mathematics not only because the child must read and write in mathematics but also mathematics itself is another entire language that is universal. The English language is essentially a set of symbols that are put together in a particular order to give them meaning; this is fundamentally exactly what mathematics is. The difference with mathematics in comparison to language is the commutative law.

The Mathematical Mind – Mathematics and the Child

> In our work, therefore, we have given a name to this part of the mind, which is built up by exactitude, we call it the mathematical mind.
> (Montessori, 1964, The Absorbent Mind)

Montessori used the term "the mathematical mind" to refer to the unique tendencies of the human mind, such as order. Montessori believed that children had an innate potential to understand and appreciate mathematics. The child is drawn to the order of mathematics. From young, the child is observing and having a sensorial relationship with their environment. It is through these experiences that the child begins to understand patterns and order. The child's mind is being developed.

The focus for the early year's child should not be about getting the right answer, rather, the process of how an answer is reached and what discoveries they make during that process. The Montessori approach lays the foundation for complete comprehension that number is quantity and size. The activities within the environment of the child have opportunities for repetition to reinforce the concepts. Montessori believed that the child would reach abstraction themselves through activities in the concrete form. By fostering a sense of autonomy, children should be afforded the opportunity to take ownership of their learning and develop confidence in their mathematical abilities.

> We have to let children experience he beauty of arithmetic . . . it is something to discover and to perceive by the hand before being understood by the mind.
>
> (Montessori, 2016a, Psychoarithmetic)

As we are aware, each child progresses at their own pace, and the mathematics curriculum should not be tied to an age or predetermined timelines. The activities within the curriculum should follow the child's readiness for each concept. A child should have the opportunity to practice math concepts until they demonstrate mastery of that concept. Mastery may come quickly for some children; others may need more time. As children in early years are still in the absorbent mind phase, it is important not to rush them through the mathematical concepts and allow them time to internalise.

Mathematics and the Adult

As part of the child's prepared environment, the adult needs to be aware of what preconceptions they bring to the environment. An absorbent mind child will automatically absorb whatever the adults impart to him, meaning they must be very careful not to exude any negative feelings that may have been accumulated over the years regarding mathematics.

Many adults, including me, received mathematics education in school based on memorisation and abstract concepts. We were taught the rules of mathematics and memorised the required tables, but not all of us fully grasped the concepts as they were presented. Many of us would have experienced that "just not getting it" feeling, yet the class still moved on to other concepts. Once we misunderstood one step in the mathematical staircase, our climb to the top became more challenging, leading to feelings of frustration, fear, and even hatred for the subject that became elusive to us.

Montessori approached mathematics completely different, ensuring the young child receives a completely sensorial introduction to the basics of math and its concepts. This experience becomes part of the child's mind without frustration; it is absorbed with joy. For many of us, math and joy would never be said together, but we have a responsibility not to discourage (even unconsciously) the child's pleasant experience with mathematics.

Young children have an opportunity to develop a love of mathematics, but it all depends on how it is presented to the child. No pressure! The child's future relationship with mathematics lies in the adult's efforts to be relaxed and pleased to work with the child in the mathematics area. We must endeavour to give the child the best impression of mathematics possible because this will then open their world to physics, biology, chemistry, and algebra.

Mathematics and the Prepared Environment

The prepared environment is crucial to the mathematics area of your setting. The order of the environment is important to allow the mathematical mind to categorise the materials. The math activities are set up in order of progression, from top to bottom and left to right of the math area. The activities for the young child offer a concrete, hands-on experience, and all activities are related to the outside world in the sense that once the child absorbs the mathematical concepts, they can see how math relates to the everyday life. This concrete experience is the foundation for future abstract work. Only when the child is ready and has a clear understanding of the concepts of the initial quantities should they be moved to abstract concepts. From when the child begins their time in your setting, you are laying the foundations for critical and creative mathematical thinking.

Mathematics is in everything we do, and mathematics is interrelated with every aspect of the prepared environment. The child's readiness and foundation for mathematics occurs in the other areas. It is the experiences in their environments that will shape the child's mathematical abilities. This is why the practical life area in early years setting is so vitally important. It is through the experience with such activities that the child develops their mathematical mind. The activities require precision, judgment, problem solving, and persistence. When a child is working with a pouring activity, they are judging how close to the other container they need to hold the jug to get the water in. They are gauging the speed they should pour to avoid any spillage. When a child is cutting paper, they are working on pattern and symmetry, or when they are planting seeds, they are working on one-to-one correspondence. These everyday life activities provide the child with opportunities for developing their independence but also provide indirect preparation for higher level math skills. The practical life activities develop orderly work habits in the child which prepares them for the need for orderly work patterns in mathematics.

This system in which a child is constantly moving objects with his hands and actively exercising his senses, also considers a child's special aptitude for mathematics. When they leave the material, the children very easily reach the point where they wish to write out the operation. They can thus carry out an abstract mental operation and acquire a kind of natural and spontaneous inclination for mental calculation.

(Montessori, 1972b, The Discovery of the Child)

Box 13.2 Lesson Example

This lesson is for an activity called spindle boxes in Montessori environments but can easily be adapted and created with resources you can access.

Purpose:
1. To clarify the idea that the symbols represent a certain quantity of separate objects or actions
2. To introduce the concept of zero
3. To reinforce the natural sequence of the numbers 1 to 9
4. Indirectly prepares for the fact that there are no other symbols other than 0–9

Age: 4 years

Materials: Two boxes divided into five compartments each, one with numerals 0–4 and the other with numerals 5–9 printed above the compartments. Forty-five spindles in a basket.

Presentation 1:
1. Invite the child to work with the spindle boxes and introduce the activity at the shelf.
2. You and the child carry one box each to the table and set them down.
3. Both return to the shelf.
4. Ask the child to carry the spindles to the table.
5. Set down and both sit down.
6. Ensure the boxes on the table are in order of 0–9 from left to right.
7. Invite the child to read the numerals from 1–9 as you point to each one.
8. You point to 1 and say it.
9. Take one spindle from the basket and count it into your hand (i.e., sat "one" as you place it in your hand).
10. Count the spindle again as you set it in the corresponding section of the box. Place the spindle in the box as noiselessly as possible.

11. Repeat steps 8–10 up to numeral 4 or 5.
12. Invite the child to finish counting and placing the remainder of the spindles into the appropriate sections of the box.
13. Once the child has completed numeral 9 and there are no remaining spindles in the basket, move on.
14. Pass your hand in the "0" compartment while asking how many spindles are in there.
15. The child will indicate there are no spindles in there.
16. Point to "0" and tell the child that zero means none.
17. Ask the child a few more questions that will elicit the response "zero" (How many spindles are in your lap? How many spindles are in the basket? etc.).
18. Invite the child to continue working with the spindle boxes or to return them to the shelf. The child is free to take out the spindle boxes anytime.

Game:

Invite two or three children who have worked with the spindle boxes independently to work together. Invite each child to do a certain number of actions (hop three times) or bring a certain number of objects (bring four flags). Ensure to include "zero" amongst your requests (bring zero pencils).

Control of error: There are exactly 45 spindles.

Figure 13.1 Spindle Boxes Activity

Box 13.3 Lesson Example

This lesson is for an activity called numerals and counters or cards and counters in Montessori environments but can easily be re-created using resources you have available.

Purpose:
1. To reinforce the knowledge that each number is made up of separate quantities.
2. To verify if the child has mastered the sequence of numbers and how many units go to form each number.
3. To visually indicate the odd and even numbers.
4. Indirect: to prepare for the divisibility of numbers.

Age: 4 years, prerequisite of spindle boxes
Materials: numerals from 1–10 and 55 counters (the counters need to all be the same)
Presentation:
1. Invite the child to work with the numerals and counters and introduce the activity at the shelf.
2. You carry the box to the table.
3. Set down and both sit down.
4. Open the box, take out the numerals, and set randomly on the table.
5. Set the box with the counters aside for now.
6. Begin to set up the numerals in a horizontal row from 1 to 10 at the top of the table, ensuring that you leave some space between ach numeral.
7. Once you have set up a few numerals, invite the child to finish the row.
8. Bring the box with the counters closer, and set out all the counters. Move the box aside.
9. Point at the numeral to the far left, and say its name (i.e., "one").
10. Count out the same number of counters aloud (i.e., "one").
11. Slide the counter(s) to just below the numeral, one at a time, counting each counter aloud.
12. Repeat steps 9–11 until you reach 5 or 6. Note: Be sure the counters are placed either directly below the numeral if odd or by twos if even (see picture later).
13. Invite the child to continue reading the numerals and placing the appropriate number of counters.
14. If the child completes "10" successfully, you can move on.
15. Run your index finger from the bottom of the counters under one numeral, upwards through the counters to the numeral, if possible.

136 *Mathematics*

Figure 13.2 Cards and Counters Activity

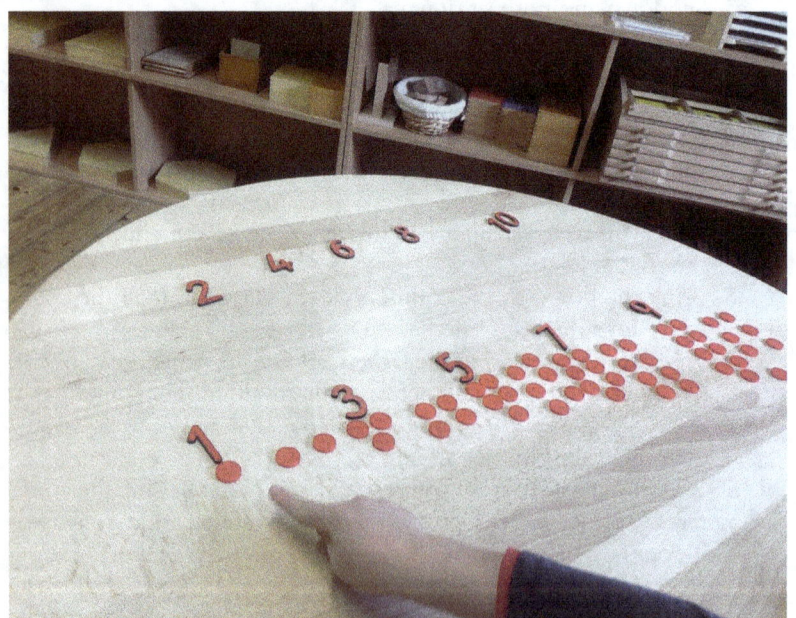

Figure 13.3 Cards and Counters Activity

16. If your finger can pass through, push the numeral you reach with your finger upward on the table.
17. This will only work for the even numerals because the off numerals have a counter in the middle of its row of counters that will prevent your finger from continuing through the counters.
18. Push up the first two or three numerals, and offer the child to push up the remainder. Once all the numerals have been pushed up, pass your hand under all the even numerals and tell the child, "These are even. Please say 'even.'"
19. Pass your hand under all the odd numerals and tell the child, "These are odd. Please say 'odd.'"
20. Push the even numbers back onto line with the odd numerals.
21. Put the activity away, and let the child know they are welcome to use this on their own.

Control of error: There are exactly 55 counters.

Encouraging a Passion for Mathematics

As with all aspects of the Montessori approach to education, Mathematics is based on the principle of hands-on and follow the child as the emergent learner. Montessori believed children need to have opportunities with activities that bring joy through a sensorial relationship with the activity. This serves as the foundation for the child's future engagement in learning.

Montessori saw mathematics as exciting but recognised that not all children felt the same. She approached mathematics with the same belief that children have a natural desire to learn. As we know, the children in our early year's settings are in the absorbent mind phase, so we want to prepare their environment with opportunities to engage with mathematical concepts:

1. Real-life opportunities: Even the youngest of children can start to explore mathematical concepts like weighing, measuring, and calculating.
2. Math is everywhere: As mentioned, it is all around us, every day. Start to discuss the connection between everyday life and mathematics with the child. Use rich language, with proper mathematical terms to explore everyday tasks with the child.
3. Explore: Young children are learning and need to learn through their own explorations. Do not focus so much on the answer; let the process be what engages the child.
4. Do not rush the child: Let them show you what they can do and where their interests are. Even when the child is struggling, offer guidance and support but encourage the child to keep trying, building their resilience.
5. Read math stories: So many texts have a mathematical aspect to their stories. Engage the child with high-quality texts that allows the child to explore mathematics in a different way.
6. Have fun with mathematics!

138 *Mathematics*

Figure 13.4 Exploring Mathematics

Figure 13.5 Exploring Mathematics

Summary

Children in our early year's settings are in the absorbent mind phase in their sensitive period for mathematics. They are in the best position to be offered opportunities to develop their mathematical mind through hands-on, concrete activities. Montessori emphasised the importance of the practical life area for embedding the foundations of mathematics for the child. Montessori also believed that children should receive a completely sensorial introduction to the basics of mathematics and its concepts.

The early years child can develop a love of mathematics, but it requires the adult to offer the activities with enjoyment and commitment. We are responsible for giving the child the best impression of mathematics as possible during these formative years. Practical life activities offer real-life and concrete activities that have an indirect purpose of introducing mathematical concepts to the young child.

14 Movement and Wellbeing

> **Box 14.1 Chapter Objectives**
>
> By the end of this chapter, you will be able to do the following:
>
> - Understand the significant role movement plays in the child's overall development of wellbeing.
> - Appreciate the importance the prepared environment plays in promoting movement and sensory exploration.
> - Understand the importance of modelling movement for the child.
> - Reflect on how much movement your setting offers the child.

Introduction

Young children need to move. Their bodies and minds are not designed to sit still. Montessori respected this in young children and advocated for movement in education. She recognised that movement plays a significant role in the child's overall wellbeing and lays the foundation for their cognitive, social, and emotional development. She highlighted the connectedness between physical and mental development and the importance of the prepared environment offering opportunities for purposeful movement and hands-on experiences to support their development. Montessori identified the child's need for movement for development of self.

> When there is motor and physical activity, you can see a more important kind of education, a kind of education that takes the force of life into account. This education is not driven by its own wisdom, but by another superior wisdom which lays down the law that, if we do not take the vital force into account, we miss the best part of education.
> (Montessori, 1946, The 1946 London Lectures)

The prepared environment (see Chapter 6) encourages a child to engage in activities that involve gross motor skills (large muscle groups) as well as fine motor skills (small muscle groups). Activities that develop a child's motor skills also support the development of concentration, coordination, hand-and-eye development, independence, and self-confidence.

Montessori believed that what the hand does, the brain remembers, and when children are given the freedom to move and explore within their environment, they develop a strong sense of self-awareness and self-regulation. This, in turn, leads to greater overall wellbeing as the child learns to navigate the world around them with confidence and resilience.

Montessori knew that children needed to move to learn, and her approach was for the child to be active within their learning. They are doers for themselves, for others, and for their environment and are all the time learning. The doing part helps the child feel connected to and understand their world around them.

> It is high time that movement came to be regarded from a new point of view in educational theory . . . as part of school life, which gives priority to the intellect, the role of movement has always been sadly neglected. When accepted there at all, it has been under the heading of "exercise," "physical development," or "games." But this is to overlook its close connection with the developing mind.
> (Montessori, 1964, The Absorbent Mind)

Box 14.2 Reflective Task

Thinking about your early years setting, how do the children respond to your requests for limited movement, such as circle time? What challenges are you facing? What feelings does this bring up for you?

Movement and the Child

Movement is essential to child development and not just in the physical or motor development, but whilst these are important, focus on the connection between motor and cognitive development was what Montessori addressed. Early years children are in a sensitive period (see Chapter 5) for movement.

> Watching a child makes it obvious that the development of his mind comes about through his movements.
> (Montessori, 1964, The Absorbent Mind)

Both fine motor skills and gross motor skills are very important. Fine motor development begins at birth, and Montessori discouraged putting the likes of mittens on babies, as she believed they should fully experience their environment with their hands. Montessori emphasised that the fine motor skills must be refined and the child's hand strengthened to prepare them for writing when older.

Montessori believed there were key benefits of movement for the young child:

- Exploration
- Sensorial development
- Motor development
- Physical development
- Concentration and focus
- Cognitive development
- Independence
- Self-discipline
- Problem solving
- Critical thinking
- Creative thinking
- Social interaction
- Communication

Montessori argued that the traditional methods of giving children a break from their "mental activity"/"work," with movements such as gymnastics, was hindering the child's development and classed it as an hinderance to the child. Montessori believed that movement without thought could lead to fatigue for the child.

The connection between the body and mind was obvious to Montessori, and she argued that it is with our body that we interact with the environment, and from this, mental growth develops. She advocated for purposeful movement in education to serve the developing mind.

> But to always be thinking about the mind on the one hand and the body on the other, is to break the continuity that should reign between them. This keeps action away from thought. But the true purpose of movement is far higher that to produce an appetite or strengthen the lungs: it is to serve the ends of existence, the universal and spiritual economies of nature.
> (Montessori, 1946, The Absorbent Mind)

Movement and Freedom

Movement and freedom are united within a Montessori environment, as Montessori believed that for the child to become independent and capable, they must be free to explore and develop. Independence and wellbeing are achieved by exploring and experiencing to create your own personal relationship with the world around you.

Montessori recognised the child's need to move and created her environments where they were free to do so. She wanted to utilise this need of the child in support of their learning, and she believed that this purposeful movement helped the child develop self-discipline and self-control. When you observe a Montessori environment, you will see movement. It is an integral part of the Montessori principles. Children are moving freely throughout the environment, free in their choice of activity, and free in their choice of where to work with that activity. Movement also enables children to encounter spontaneous interactions with their peers, developing their social and emotional skills.

Montessori recognised that by incorporating freedom of movement within the prepared environment, movement of thought developed into concentration, independence, and resilience,

Movement and the Adult

> Every complex action is made up of successive incidents, one quite distinct from the other; one act follows another. Trying to recognise and to execute exactly and separately these successive acts is the analysis of movement.
> (Montessori, 1972b, The Discovery of the Child)

The adult breaks down each movement of the activities when giving the lesson to the child. They are purposeful, exact, and meaningful in their own movement for the child to absorb this task. There is a purposeful lack of language in most activities initially (except where language is required – e.g., letter sounds) for the child to focus on the movement and not get distracted. If we are talking, the child will focus on our lips moving rather than our hands.

> The adult must be always calm and act slowly so that all the details of his actions may be clear to the child who is watching.
> (Montessori, 1977, The Secret of Childhood)

When we think of the newborn baby and reflect on their ability to learn through movement and their sensorial experiences, we encourage such movement. We champion for the infant to move, yet when they can move, we impose restrictions! The infant starts out with tracking objects with their eyes, later touching, grasping, and manipulating with their hands. Through these movements, they gain the control of their body and the ability to meet their own needs. Montessori argued that we then "cage" the child with the intention of protecting them from harm but is more as a convenience to the adult, which is robbing the child of opportunities for development.

Montessori believed the adult should never be the focus of the environment. They should not be at the front of the environment with the expectation that children remain focused on them. They should move, with intent, around the environment, observing the children, providing lessons, offering opportunities for purposeful movement and exploration, but all time ensuring not to disturb or dictate the work of the child. Purposeful movement is at the core of Montessori, and we facilitate this with the preparation of the activities in the prepared environment. The movement we refer to is movement that connects the mind and the body.

> Never give more to the mind than you give to the hand.
> (Montessori, 1946, The Absorbent Mind)

Movement and the Prepared Environment

The prepared environment, as previously addressed, welcomes movement for the child. The design and layout consider and facilitate the child's need to move. The shelving and furniture are all designed for the child to be successful in their movement, independent of the adult.

> Movement of the hand is essential. Little children revealed that the development of the mind is stimulated by the movement of the hands. The hand is the instrument of the intelligence. The child needs to manipulate objects to gain experience by touching and handling
> (Montessori, 1946, The London Lectures)

The activities are didactic for the child to incorporate all their senses in their learning processes. The child has the freedom to observe the movement of others, explore the prepared environment, and refine their senses as they absorb their environment. The environment enriches the child's opportunity to be an active learner rather than passive. The prepared environment should be an ecosystem for stimulating the child's senses. For this to be effective, the environment is carefully organised, with activities positioned on child-accessible shelving, promoting focus and calmness. The environment does not require the child to request permission to move around. The child chooses their work and chooses either to work at a table or on a rug on the floor.

Everything within the environment is tailored to the child, from safety to accessibility, and the activities offered play a huge part in supporting the child's need to move. Practical life activities are the foundation for movement within the environment and should be prioritised throughout the child's time in your environment. Montessori stated that it was the repetition of the movement within practical life activities that builds the connection between mind and body (see example lesson later). Whilst these activities are the foundation, all activities, from sensorial to language to mathematics to art, should involve the child doing and moving. For example, in Montessori environments, the children learn the letter sounds by tracing the sandpaper letters. They are moving to learn.

Box 14.3 Activity Example: Boxes and Bottles

Focus: Movement of the adult within the practical life lesson of opening and closing different containers broken down into steps. Reflect on the precise movements within this activity as it is presented to the child.
Purpose: 1. Control and coordination of movement. 2. Preparation for opening and closing different boxes and bottles.
Age: 2.5–3 years
Materials: one large container, mat, variety of boxes, and bottles with different closures

Presentation:

1. Invite the child to work with you, and introduce the child to the activity at the shelf.
2. Carrying the mat for boxes and bottles: show the child how to carry the mat for boxes and bottles; the mat is carried vertical to the body, one fist over top of the other.
3. Set the mat down on the self, and invite the child to take the mat.
4. Pick up the container, placing all four fingers underneath and thumbs on top of the container.
5. Walk with the child to the table.
6. Invite the child to set the mat on the table and then set the container on the table.
7. Both you and the child sit down.
8. Set the container aside to the top right of the table.
9. <u>Unrolling the mat</u>: The rolled mat should be perpendicular to the child's and your body. The exposed edge of the mat should be on the right side. Place your right hand on the right edge of the mat and hold firmly. With left hand, unroll the mat towards the child's side of the table.
10. Use pencil grip to grasp the bottom left and right corners with corresponding hands. Flip the mat over, and smooth it out with both hands.
11. With two hands, pick up the container, and set the container on the tale to the top centre of the mat.
12. With your left hand on the base of the container, use your right hand to open the lid of the container so the child can see what is inside.
13. Setting out the boxes and bottles: With your right hand, remove the boxes and bottles from the container one by one. Be sure to handle the boxes and bottles by grasping the body of the boxes and bottles and not the lids. Set each down in the centre of the mat.

14. With your left hand on the base of the container, use your right hand to close the lid of the container. With two hands, pick up the container, and set it back to the top right side of the table.
15. <u>Opening the boxes and bottles</u>: With your left hand, pick up one box or bottle by the body, and place it on the front and centre of the mat. While holding the box or bottle with your left hand, use your right hand to remove its lid. Place the lid to the far right of the mat and then place the body of the box or bottle to the far left of the mat.
16. Repeat step 15 for all the remaining boxes and bottles.
17. <u>Closing boxes and bottles</u>: With your left hand, pick up one box or bottle, and place it to the front and centre of the mat. Take a moment to visually scan the lids to see which one will fit this box or bottle (even if you already know which one will fit). With your right hand, pick up the appropriate lid, and place the lid on the body of the box or bottle, using whatever method the box or bottle dictates for its closing (i.e. turning, pushing, sliding, etc.). Place the closed box with lid on the back centre of the mat.
18. Repeat step 17 for the remining boxes and bottles.
19. With two hands, pick up the container, and set the container to the top centre of the mat.
20. With your left hand on the base of the container, use your right hand to open the lid.
21. Putting away boxes and bottles: replace the boxes into the container, one by one, using the right hand, picking the boxes and bottles up by the body until they are all returned to the container.
22. With your left hand on the base of the container, use your right hand to close the lid of the container. With two hands, pick up the container, and set it to the top right side of the table.
23. <u>Rolling the mat:</u> Using a pencil grip, grasp the bottom left and right corners with corresponding hands. Flip the mat over.
24. Place your right hand directly in the centre of the mat, and rotate the mat 90 degrees clockwise so the short side of the mat is closest to the child and yourself.
25. With a pencil grip, grasp the bottom left and right corners with corresponding hands, and begin to roll up the mat. Pause periodically and check to see that the edges of the mat are lining up (touch or tap both edges with the index and middle finger). Continue rolling the mat until it is completely rolled up.

Movement and Wellbeing 147

26. Place the mat directly in front of the child. With two hands, pick up the container, and set the container directly in front of the child.
27. Invite the child to do the activity.

Points of Interest: the different closures on the boxes and bottles
Notes:

1. Make sure you have child-sized boxes and bottles.
2. Clean out the boxes and bottles thoroughly; remove labels and stickers.
3. Make sure there are a variety of closures.
4. Make sure all lids come away from the body of the box or bottle.
5. Make sure your boxes and bottles are not all the same texture, weight, or colour.

Figure 14.1 Boxes and Bottles Activity

Box 14.4 Reflective Task

How are you teaching letter sounds within your environment?

The sandpaper lesson activity is to aid the child in learning the letter sounds. There is no requirement to purchase specialised Montessori equipment for this. Use the resources you have to create this activity.

The movement connection for the child between feeling the shape of the letter when hearing the sound. The tactile work of repeatedly tracing the letters, made of sandpaper, whilst saying the sound gives the child a muscular memory of the letter sound. This embodies the concept that language is multi-sensory for the child.

Now take this activity and create even more movement by placing the letters across the room on a table or rug. The adult will ask the child to bring specific letter sound. The child moves between the two spaces at the same time as developing their focus and concentration.

How can you incorporate movement and a tactile experience for the child in your environment as they learn the letter sounds?

Figure 14.2 Sandpaper Letters Activities

Movement and Wellbeing 149

Figure 14.3 Sandpaper Letters Activities

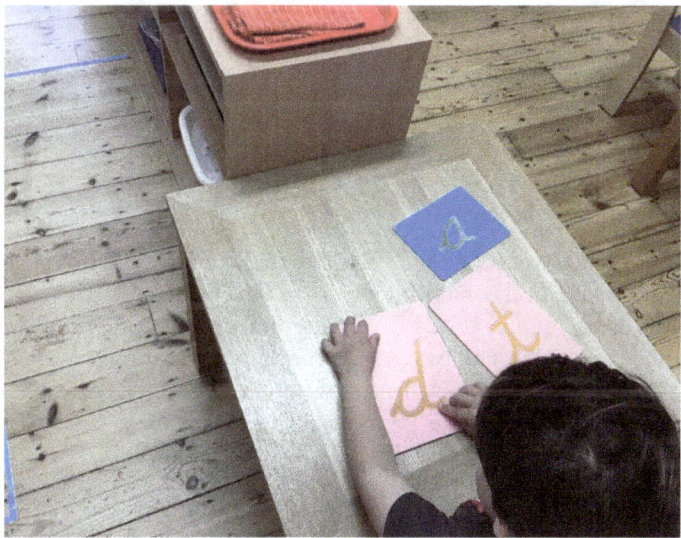

Figure 14.4 Sandpaper Letters Activities

Movement and Sports

Montessori's approach to working with children to support development of movement can be applied to all movement opportunities for children, including sport. Considering the awareness of the child learning through hands-on experiences, this can easily be applied to sport. The benefit of sport is well-known for being more than the physical benefit.

Participation in sport affords the child with the same opportunities as the prepared environment within early years settings, such as the opportunity to develop their collaboration, resilience, perseverance, discipline, and respect. Bringing Montessori philosophy and sport together also nurtures the whole development of the child.

> Tennis, football and the like does not have for their sole purpose the accurate moving of a ball, but they challenge us to acquire a new skill – something lacking before – and this feeling of enhancing our abilities is the real source of delight in the game.
> (Montessori, 1964, The Absorbent Mind)

Sport is believed to be a universal appeal for children. Lack of movement is detrimental for children, and we live in a society now where movement is removed as a priority in place of more sedentary lifestyle, even in education. This needs to change for the sake of the future of our children's mental health and wellbeing.

Viewing sport as a concrete experience rather than the traditional view of physical education will enable the incorporation of the Montessori principles easily and will enhance the child's development of self-direction, concentration, self-worth, teamwork, etc., as well as build a healthy approach to sportsmanship and respect, which is in all aspects of the Montessori approach already. It also prepares the child for a healthy approach to competition which will enhance their own drive to reach their own potential and protect their wellbeing.

Movement and Wellbeing

Montessori embodies respect and care for the child and prepares the whole child for life in all aspects of its philosophy and practice which protects a child's wellbeing from a young age. Early priority of protecting one's own wellbeing can become daily habits and part of everyday life even for our young children. Montessori meets wellbeing in the following areas, and movement is embedded throughout:

- Spiritual
- Emotional
- Social
- Physical

How often do we hear the importance of physical movement for our overall wellbeing? Physical activity is promoted as the key factor for supporting our mental health and mental wellbeing. For children, this isn't just about the specialised physical education; it is the everyday movement, and they need opportunities throughout their day to be active, even when not engaged in a sports or gym class.

Montessori believed that offering children an opportunity to participate in exercises of muscular education will support their development of physiological movements, mastering ordinary skills of life.

> When there is motor and physical activity, you can see a more important kind of education, a kind of education that takes the force of life into account.
> (Montessori, 1946, The London Lectures)

Summary

Movement matters!

Montessori respected the child's need to move but also understand the value in each movement and advocated for recognition of the relationship between the mind and the body. The freedom of movement comes from the prepared environment offering purposeful movement opportunities. Movement is essential in learning and can be the fuel for development, but it is also necessary in the development of discipline. Children are not designed to sit still; they have an internal need to move, and it is through these movements that they become focused and concentrated.

Montessori recognised the role of purposeful movement and physical activity in promoting learning, development, and overall wellbeing. She also recognised movement as essential for cognitive, social, and emotional growth in young children. All aspects of the Montessori approach embody movement. Movement is a natural and essential component of the learning process, stimulating the neural pathways, supporting brain development, and enhancing cognitive functions.

15 Social and Emotional Development

> **Box 15.1 Chapter Overview**
>
> By the end of this chapter, you will be able to do the following:
>
> - Explore how building positive social skills from a young age supports the overall development of the child.
> - Understand the value of grace and courtesy activities within your setting in supporting social and emotional wellbeing.
> - Explore how the social interactions contribute to the child's emotional wellbeing, self-esteem, and self-regulation.
> - Appreciate your role and the role of the prepared environment in fostering social and emotional development.

Introduction

The Montessori approach is often viewed as the focus is mostly on the development of the individual rather than a social being. This is a very superficial impression, as Montessori recognised the importance of the child's social development, but she recognised the link between the child as an individual and the child as a social being.

Montessori emphasised the importance of viewing the child's growth and development from a place of love, creating a nurturing and respectful environment where children are free to develop their social and emotional skills.

For many children, nursery is the first opportunity for them to expand their social community wider than their family and family friends. They begin to be exposed to the behaviour of others and how that may impact them. To begin with, adults must be aware of their own concept of social. For a child, it is looks different from how adults view it. The early years child is at the start of building their social self. Early years children are still learning to understand their emotions and finding their place within their communities.

DOI: 10.4324/9781003466970-16

Montessori recognises that when young children are attuned to their emotions, they become capable of understanding themselves and others. Montessori believed that the holistic development of a child stems far beyond the academic achievements to encompass their social and emotional wellbeing. The importance of fostering strong social connections, emotional intelligence, and resilience from the earlier stages of a child's life is incorporated throughout the Montessori method.

The trilogy of the child, the adult, and the environment is very relevant here also, focusing on interpersonal and social skills:

- Care of self
- Care of others
- Care of the environment

Montessori believed that children offered the hope for a more peaceful world. With each generation brings new hope. Unfortunately, it is common practice in traditional settings to separate peace education rather than embedding it within all aspects of education.

> There is among children an evident sense of community. This rests on the noblest feelings and creates unity in the group. These examples are enough to teach us that under conditions in which the emotional life reaches a high level, and the children's personalities are normalised, a kind of attraction makes itself felt.
> (Montessori, 1964, The Absorbent Mind)

Understanding Social Development

In Montessori, social development is nurtured through the prepared environment, collaboration, exploration, and discovery opportunities and from the role of the adult. Children learn to be an active member within their community in a respectful way. They learn to communicate effectively, resolve conflicts peacefully, and develop empathy and compassion towards others.

Fostering Emotional Intelligence

Our young children have yet to develop the ability to control their emotions. In conjunction with neural, cognitive, and behavioural growth, emotional development occurs. Central to the Montessori approach is the cultivation of emotional intelligence and the ability to recognise, understand, and manage one's own emotions as well as those of others. The prepared environment affords children the opportunities to explore and express their feelings and develop the language to identify their emotions.

The adults model empathy and active listening but also create a safe and supportive environment where children are valued, heard, and understood.

Montessori believed in empowering children by validating their emotions and supporting them with constructive coping strategies. This helps them to navigate their emotions with confidence and resilience.

Promoting a Culture of Respect

Every aspect of the Montessori environment is infused with respect. Children are respected and in turn learn to respect themselves, others, and their environment. The grace and courtesy activities foster respect throughout the environment, laying the foundation for positive relationships and interactions.

Social and Emotional Development and the Child

- Value their own individuality
- Work in collaboration with others
- Grace and courtesy

The mixed-age environments are a signature element of Montessori environments, and although not all settings can provide this, the benefits are clear. Montessori recognised that children are quick to learn from one another, growing together naturally. Children will interact with children older and younger, with different abilities and interests, much like how we do in our everyday life as adults.

Within a mixed-age environment, there is less pressure to compete, and the focus becomes the collaboration, support, and assistance with one another. They form a community that re-creates that family structure.

Montessori recognised that the emergence of a social awareness occurs in the absorbent mind phase when a child is between 3 and 6 years. Young children may have outbursts or feel frustrated when trying to understand and manage their own emotions, but we need to remember, this is normal. It is even necessary for them to develop the ability to be perceptive, allowing them to understand others.

Social and emotional development work together; as the young children are developing their abilities to be patient, communicate, and collaborate, they are developing their ability to self-regulate and interact with others. Children are forming their community within the carefully prepared environment. This period of a child's life is crucial for laying the foundation for emotional intelligence. Developing strong social and emotional skills during these early years fosters resilience and aids in their ability to navigate the complexities of later social interactions.

Social and Emotional Development and the Adult

> We must study the profound and mysterious psychology of the little child, observe its development, and find what we can do to help.
> (Montessori, 1946, The London Lectures)

The adult as the facilitator is important to remember here. We know it is a unique component of the Montessori approach where the adult guides rather than dictates. The adult guides children towards activities, experiences, and opportunities for exploration that will support them in their social and emotional development. They do provide the support, encouragement, and guidance throughout the child's journey.

> When adults interfere in this first stage of preparation for social life, they nearly always make mistakes.
> (Montessori, 1964, The Absorbent Mind)

When the child is working through their social development, we often feel the immense urge to intervene, but ultimately, we inevitably disrespect the child. When we rush to the rescue unnecessarily, we are telling the child that we do not trust them to problem solve for themselves.

Children benefit when they build positive relationships with the adults in their lives. Adults play a crucial role in fostering children's social and emotional development by modelling empathy and respect in their own interactions with others. Setting positive examples of respect, patience, kindness, and understanding helps the child develop their social and emotional skills.

Developing an environment that encourages children to take ownership of their own learning experiences, giving them freedom to choose, make decisions, and evaluate their own progress, develops a sense of empowerment, autonomy, and responsibility. This supports the child to develop self-awareness, self-esteem, and emotional wellbeing.

Using your observational skills, you will be able to recognise the challenges children encounter when developing their social and emotional skills and respond with love, patience, and guidance, according to their need. Life moves at a rapid pace, and often, we miss the signs that children are struggling if we do not take the time to slow down and observe. It is important for children to feel heard and seen.

Social and Emotional Development and the Prepared Environment

Building a sense of community within the prepared environment supports the development of the social and emotional child. Montessori highlighted that we must consider the child from the point of view of love and noted that children have no control over what condition of life they are born into nor do they care, but they do need a loving environment. We know how much the child is developing in the early years, and their needs quickly move from a foundation of love into the need of a supportive and social environment.

> The child's progress does not depend only on his age, but also on being free to look about him.
> (Montessori, 1964, The Absorbent Mind)

Montessori observed that children in the first plane, the birth-to-age-6 child, are working on the development of their entire being. The mixed ages within early years environments really support the social and emotional development of the child. The social foundation developed during this phase will support them later in life with family, friends, work, and communities. Children learn from one another. Older children are role models and become leaders within their community, supporting and assisting the younger children. The younger children go to the older children for guidance and support but also to observe what they themselves can achieve one day. This togetherness as they grow is natural and nurtured within the environment.

> To segregate by age is one of the cruellest and most inhuman things one can do.
> (Montessori, 1964, The Absorbent Mind)

Self-regulation is necessary to ensure the child can control their own emotions. Rather than the reward-punishment system, Montessori focuses on the intrinsic motivation of the child. Through grace and courtesy lessons, children are learning appropriate communication of their feelings and wishes and are learning how to interact and engage socially in a respectful manner. The grace and courtesy lessons instil manners, respect, and empathy in young children, supporting them developing their social interactions with confidence and respect for themselves and others.

Fostering freedom of choice in their prepared environment supports the social and emotional development of the child. Montessori explored this, discussing the number of activities we offer the child, and highlighted the negative impact it can have when we offer too much. Montessori believed that by having more than one set of material, we were in fact robbing children of the opportunity to develop maturity and patience, necessary in their social lives.

> For if there are too many things, or more than one complete set for a group of thirty or forty children, this causes confusion. So, we have few things, even if there are many children.
> (Montessori, 1964, The Absorbent Mind)

Peace Education

> An education capable of saving humanity is no small undertaking; it involves the spiritual development of man, the enhancement of his value as an individual, and the preparation of young people to understand the times in which they live.
> (Montessori, 1992a, Education and Peace)

Peace education is a major aspect of the Montessori method and goes together with grace and courtesy within the prepared environment. Children are given lessons from how to greet someone to resolving conflict respectfully. The grace and courtesy activities can be planned or spontaneous, but during the early stages of the child's transition to their new environment, it is necessary to focus on the activities that will support the child's independence and foster a sense of belonging, such as the following:

- How to walk in the environment
- How to ask for help
- How to interrupt
- How to carry activities to a table or rug
- How to unroll and roll a rug
- How to ask to work with someone or observe someone working

These simply and quick lessons give the child the tools they need to navigate their environment and engage socially with adults and peers. Grace and courtesy lessons require no specific material on the shelf, but they are vitally important in maintaining a harmonious environment where everyone works together. It is important to acknowledge that providing an environment focused on peace education does not mean there is an absence of conflict. We are working with young children who are developing their individuality; of course, there will be conflict!

Montessori's life spanned two world wars. This made her more determined to advocate for the peace education, starting in early years. The first plane of development, children have a sensitive period to language, and one aspect of peace education and social and emotional development is acquiring the words to use to articulate emotions and feelings.

> There is among children an evident sense of community. This rests on the noblest feelings and creates unity in the group. These examples are enough to teach us that under conditions in which the emotional life reaches a high level, and the children's personalities are normalised, a kind of attraction makes itself felt.
> (Montessori, 1964, The Absorbent Mind)

Summary

At the core of Montessori philosophy is peace education, fostering the child's social and emotional development, rooted in respect and love. Montessori believed that children were the change agents needed for a more harmonious world, and to achieve this, we much begin in the early years of their lives.

Social and emotional development should form part of the everyday interactions and embedded across all aspects of the curriculum, not separate and isolated. Fostering confident, independent, and capable individuals requires education that goes beyond academics and meets the needs of the whole child. This holistic approach prepares a child to be citizens of change and citizens of the world.

16 Making It Work in Your Environment

Now that you have read the book, you will be looking at how you can incorporate the Montessori principles into your setting. Every setting is different and serve different communities, and this book has been written in a way that you can easily adapt the principles to work for you. Just remember: FOLLOW THE CHILD!

Before you rush and change everything all at once, I recommend you reflect as a team on how you will work together to incorporate these changes. Children need consistency, and if the adults in the environment are not all offering the same practice, this will cause confusion and frustration for the child.

Reflective Questions for the Team

1. Do you believe the child will show you what they need?
2. Do you understand the benefits of Montessori for young children?
3. How do you currently support the children's learning?
4. Do you observe the children? What do you do with these observations?
5. Do you understand how to "follow the child"?
6. How do you enable child to construct their own learning?
7. How can the environment you provide support them in this?
8. How important is the role of order and structure in enabling children's discoveries?
9. What everyday tasks might be shared with children to promote responsibility and feelings of competence?
10. Do you have a practical life area?
11. How do you support children to develop self-discipline
12. How might you support children to use movement and manipulation of resources to explore ideas more fully?
13. What kinds of observation provide you with the level of detail you need about children's thinking, learning, and development?

Montessori urges us to be conscious in our preparation of self when we work with child. Being reflective and asking where you stand now is necessary to be able to truly serve the needs of the child. The previous section is just an example of questions you might want to start with. Working through the planes of development, the absorbent mind, and the sensitive periods together will embed consistency amongst the team. Take the time to familiarise yourself with the characteristics of these stages of development.

Understanding the significance of incorporating Montessori principles into your education framework to support the holistic development of the child is necessary for the effectiveness of this approach. Throughout this book, there is a clear message on the importance of early ears in future learning; it also highlights that children have the greatest capacity to learn between the ages of birth to 6.

Practical Application of the Montessori Principles

1. Observation: Observation is key to understanding the child. Montessori stated that we should first observe and then guide the child. Observation will give you an insight into the child's development stage, sensitive period, interests, and choices. These will support you in meeting the child's needs with appropriate activities and in preparation of the environment.
2. Prepared environment: Montessori referred to all aspects of the environment as the prepared environment, not just the physical space. The overall layout, preparation, arrangement, and presentation of the activities are considered central to the needs of the child. The environment is equipped with accessible furnishings and the activities displayed in reach of the child.
3. Hands-on: The activities offer the child a hands-on experience across all areas of the curriculum. The foundation being the activities in the practical life area that offer activities that promote focus and concentration, hand-eye coordination, motor development, social and emotional development, and confidence.
4. Grace and courtesy: Children are not born knowing how to be in their world. Lessons in grace and courtesy foster respect, social and emotional development, and a sense of belonging and responsibility.
5. Freedom within limits: The environment offers the child the freedom to move, choose, make mistakes, and be independent which encompasses trust and respect for the child. Without the freedom of choice, children cannot learn to be independent and make decisions.
6. Understand the principles – read the book!

Working With Families

Montessori recognised the value in working with parents and supporting them to understand what Montessori has to offer was essential to her work. Children benefit from the positive relationships between early years settings and their families. We are in a position to build communities, and today, our society needs this. Many parents are juggling to balance work and home and are faced with time that is often rushed with their children. Others are alone in their parenting and lack their own wider families for support and guidance. We can help parents understand their child's development needs, supporting them to become more confident in their own role. Despite my own training and knowledge, I have questioned my own parenting at times and have needed the support of others.

Throughout this book, I have addressed the importance of observation but didn't go into depth about the value of having parents observe their own children in the classroom. This needs careful consideration before implementing this. Consideration for all children and their needs is required. At one of my schools, I put observation windows in every classroom. These were one-way to not disturb the children and worked well for parents of very small children. They were able to observe their child without the fear of upsetting them. Observation is a skill that I would encourage families to learn as well.

Parent education also brings parents into the Montessori community. Share your knowledge. Host parent education sessions and take one area of development or the environment and explore it with them in greater depth. The more the parents see what you are doing and how it helps their child, the more likely they are to continue this at home. The children themselves will most likely display the traits of what they are learning in school at home, and parents want to know more! Parents come from a place of wanting the best for their child, and we should approach our relationships with families from a place of love, respect, and understanding.

Is Montessori for All Children?

I get asked this question a lot. My go-to response has always been "yes," Montessori is suitable for all children, but I do add it is not always suitable for all families or all situations with children.

Montessori provides a supportive environment for children of all abilities. We already know that Montessori recognised that children learn at their own pace and respects their individual learning journey. Within a Montessori environment, all children are free from the pressure of expected progress at a certain age or time-specific goals. We follow the child.

Through observation, we will know how to meet the child's needs, but it is our responsibility to educate ourselves further on needs we are not familiar with. If a child struggles in a traditional setting, there is no guarantee that they won't struggle in a Montessori environment. There may be a difference in how we approach the needs of the child, but their needs do not disappear.

Montessori began her work with children living in a challenging socio-economic situation and considered to have disruptive behaviours due to a range of reasons. Montessori provides an environment where all children can access the best possible education and care, supporting them to become confident within their own potential.

The various aspects of Montessori education explored throughout this book benefit all children. Giving children the freedom to lead their own learning journey develops self-confidence, resilience, independence, and a sense of belonging. It also meets their innate drive to learn and fosters self-belief in their own capabilities.

What Next?

We are all learning about young children, some at different stages of that learning. Today with new research on child development, neuroscience, and the importance of early years, it is clear Montessori was ahead of her time. We are still fighting for the same changes she envisioned over 150 years ago.

We can continue to complain and nothing changes, or we stop complaining and be active in making change happen. We owe it to our children to fight for their future, and together, we stand stronger. Challenge your governments, your policy makers, and your stakeholders in education and childcare. We are the experts on early childhood, so we need to be louder in our call to action. We need to demand that children are central to all decisions made about them.

This book is not the solution, but I do hope it is the spark that ignites your drive and passion to embed change where necessary for the benefit of children.

Figure 16.1 Follow the Child!

162 *Making It Work in Your Environment*

Figure 16.2 Follow the Child!

I hope it inspires you to be reflective of yourself and your own practice and always strive to do the best by the child, and finally, I hope this book is an aid for you on your journey to following the child.

> The child is both a hope and a promise for mankind.
> (Montessori, 1992a, Education and Peace)

Bibliography

Eissler, T. (2009) Montessori Madness: A Parent to Parent Argument for Montessori Education. Sevenoff.
Epstein, P. (1995) "The Montessori Method: Informed by Observation." The National Montessori Reporter, Vol. 19, No. 3, pp. 14–15.
Feez, S. (2009) Montessori and Early Childhood: A Guide for Students. SAGE Publications.
Issacs, B. (2010) Bringing the Montessori Approach to Your Early Years Practice. Taylor & Francis.
Issacs, B. (2018) Understanding the Montessori Approach: Early Years Education in Practice. Routledge.
Kramer, R. (2017) Maria Montessori: A Biography. Diversion Books.
Lillard, A. S. (2017) Montessori: The Science Behind the Genius. Oxford University Press.
Lillard, P. P. (1973) Montessori: A Modern Approach. Knopf Doubleday Publishing Group.
Lillard, P. P. (2011) Montessori Today: A Comprehensive Approach to Education from Birth to Adulthood. Knopf Doubleday Publishing Group.
Lillard, P. P. (2013) Montessori in the Classroom: A Teachers Account of How Children Really Learn. Knopf Doubleday Publishing Group.
Lillard, P. P. & Jessen, L. L. (2008) Montessori from the Start: The Child at Home, from Birth to Age Three. Knopf Doubleday Publishing Group.
McTamaney, C. (2007) The Tao of Montessori: Reflection on Compassionate Teaching. iUniverse Publishing.
Montessori, M. (1914) Maria Montessori: A Centenary Anthology 1870–1970. Association Montessori Internationale (first published in 1970).
Montessori, M. (1946) The 1946 London Lectures. Montessori Pierson Publishing Company.
Montessori, M. (1949) The Absorbent Mind. Theosophical Publishing House.
Montessori, M. (1963) Education for a New World. Kalakshetra Publications.
Montessori, M. (1964) The Absorbent Mind. Theosophical Press.
Montessori, M. (1965a) Spontaneous Activity in Education: The Advances Montessori Method. Schocken Books (first published in 1917).
Montessori, M. (1965b) Dr. Montessori's Own Handbook: A Short Guide to Her Ideas and Materials. Knopf Doubleday Publishing Group.
Montessori, M. (1967) The Absorbent Mind. Kalakshetra Publications.
Montessori, M. (1971) The Four Planes of Education. Association Montessori Internationale.
Montessori, M. (1972a) The Secret of Childhood. Random House Publishing Group.

Montessori, M. (1972b) The Discovery of the Child. Random House Publishing Group.
Montessori, M. (1977) The Secret of Childhood. Orient Longman Publishing.
Montessori, M. (1986) The Discovery of the Child. Clio Press.
Montessori, M. (1989a) The Child in the Family. Clio Press.
Montessori, M. (1989b) The Child, Society and the World: Unpublished Speeches and Writings. Clio Press.
Montessori, M. (1989c) Education for a New World. Clio Press.
Montessori, M. (1989d) What You Should Know about Your Child. Clio Press.
Montessori, M. (1989e) The Formation of Man. Clio Press.
Montessori, M. (1992a) Education and Peace. Clio Press.
Montessori, M. (1992b) Education for Human Development: Understanding Montessori. Clio Press.
Montessori, M. (1996) From Childhood to Adolescence: Including "Erdkinder" and the Function of the University. Clio Press.
Montessori, M. (2007a) To Educate the Human Potential. Montessori-Pierson Publishing Co.
Montessori, M. (2007b) Maria Montessori Speaks to Parents: A Selection of Articles. Montessori-Pierson Publishing Co.
Montessori, M. (2007c) Psychogeometry. Montessori-Pierson Publishing Co.
Montessori, M. (2008) From Childhood to Adolescence. Montessori-Pierson Publishing Co.
Montessori, M. (2012) The 1946 London Lectures. Montessori-Pierson Publishing Co.
Montessori, M. (2016a) Psychoarithmetic: Arithmetic Developed under the Guidance Outlined by Child Psychology. Montessori-Pierson Publishing Co.
Montessori, M. (2016b) "Observation and Development from Dr. Montessori's 1946 London Training Course." NAMTA Journal, Vol. 41, No. 3.
Montessori, M. (2019) Citizen of the World. Montessori-Pierson Publishing Co.
Murray, A., Tebano-Ahlquist, E. M., McKenna, M., & Debs, M. (2023) The Bloomsbury Handbook of Montessori Education. Bloomsbury Publishing.
Slade, E. (2021) Montessori in Action: Building Resilient Montessori Schools. Wiley Press.
Snyder, J. R. (2014) Tending the Light. Essays on Montessori Education.
Standing, E. M. (2008) Maria Montessori Her Life and Work. Cosmo Publications.

Index

Note: Page numbers in *italics* indicate figures.

absorbent mind 8, 34–35; and adult 40–41; capability of 40; case study 41–42; and child 39–40; conscious 35, 37, 39–40; foundation for future personality 40; and mathematics 130–131, 137; phases 35, 42–43; plane of 36–37, 42–43, 157; and prepared environment 41; responsibility 40–41; unconscious 36, 37, 39
absorption of environment, child 38–39
active learning 83, 84
adult 14; absorbent mind and 40–41; freedom within limits and 79–80; hands-on learning and 87–88; independence and 100–101; language and 119; mathematics and 131–132; movement and 143–144; observation and 22, 24–25, *33*; play and 66–67; prepared environment and 52, 57–58; presentations 16; respect and 109; role 9, 15; sensitive periods and 48–49; social and emotional development 154–155
age of play 64; *see also* play
"aid to life" 13, 97
autonomy: and empowerment 97; and freedom of choice 78; independence and 102

beauty, prepared environment 17, 53
boxes and bottles activity, movement 145–147, *147*

Casa dei Bambini (Children's House) 6
case study: absorbent mind 41–42; independence in setting table 104–106, *105*; observation 81–82; respect, child's individual 112–113
child developement stages 14
Children's House (Casa dei Bambini) 6
child-sized prepared environment 17, 59; *see also* prepared environment
communication 81, 119
conscious absorbent mind 35, 37; cognitive and developmental capacities 39; features of 40; opportunities for exploration and discovery 39
consistency of language 130
counters activity 135–137, *136*

direct observation: of child 26; of self 26; *see also* observation
directress/director *see* adult

emotional development 152–157
emotional intelligence 153–154
empowerment 97
encouragement: passion for mathematics 137; and praise 111
executive functioning skills 97

fabrics matching activity, hands-on learning 84–85, *86*
first plane of development *see* plane of absorbent mind (0–6 years)
"follow the child" 7, 12, 19, 23, 108, 158, *161*, *162*
freedom 53, 57, 77; of choice 18, 78, 81, 156; of collaboration 78; independence and self-reliance 78; to make mistakes 81; of movement

78, 81, 142–144, 151; of repetition 78; and responsibility 76, 78; of time 78, 81
freedom within limits 9, 18, 57, 76–78, 159; and adult 79–80; communication and 81; expectations setting 80; holistic development 78–79; individual guidance and support 78; in practice 81; and prepared environment 80–81; respect for environment 77; respect for oneself 77; respect for others 77

Garden City Montessori School 112–113
grace and courtesy lessons 111–112, 156–157, 159; on blowing your nose 113–114, *114*

hands-on learning/experience 8, 40, 59, 83–84, 159; adult and child learning 87; and child 84–86; concrete understanding 86; fabrics matching activity 84–85, *86*; independence in setting table 104–106, *105*; and motoric memory 87; movement and (*see* movement); practical life activities and 89, *89–92*, 92–95, *94*; and prepared environment 88–89; tactile sense development 84–85
holistic development 78–79, 153

independence 96; and adult 100–101; and autonomous development 102; case study 104–106; and child 97–98, *98–100*; and life skills 77; and prepared environment 18, 101–102; promotion 97; self-confidence and 98; in setting table 104–106, *105*; and uninterrupted work periods 103–104; and wellbeing 142–143
indirect observation 26; *see also* observation
individuality of child 12–14; respect 108–109, 112–113
instilling a love of reading 127–128
intangible environment, language and 120
intellectual environment 53
interpersonal and social skills 153

language: activities 58; and adult 119; and child 118–119; intangible environment 120; and mathematics 130; and prepared environment 119–123, *120–123*; sensitive periods for 46–47, 117, 118; tangible environment 119; three-period lesson 123–125
learning: active 83–84; hands-on (*see* hands-on learning/experience); play with 63–66
left-to-right progression, prepared environment 18

mathematics 59; absorbent mind phase for 131, 137; and adult 131–132; child mathematical mind 129–131; consistency of language 130; encouraging passion for 137; exploration in 137, *138*; formal 130; informal 129–130; numerals and counters activity 135–137, *136*; origin 129; and prepared environment 132–133; presentation pattern in 130; sensorial introduction to 132; spindle boxes activity 133–134, *134*
mixed-age grouping/environments 9, 154, 156
Montesano, G. 5
Montessori education 6, 11, 160–161; challenges 10; child at the centre of the approach 9; child developement stage 14; current landscape of 10–11; experience and advocacy 1–2; grace and courtesy lessons 111–114, *114*, 156–157, 159; mathematics (*see* mathematics); observation (*see* observation); outdoor play 70–72, *72–74*, 74; philosophical approach 7, 12; play (*see* play); social and emotional development 152–157; sustainability 11; tactile sense development 84–85; uninterrupted work periods 103–104; working with families 159–160
Montessori, M. 1, 2, 39, 44, 45, 142; challenges 6; concepts of absorbent mind 34; early career in medicine 11; life and work 4–6; observation 6; philosophical foundations 7
Montessori principles 2–3, 7–10, 158–159; absorbent mind (*see* absorbent mind); child at centre of approach 9; freedom (*see* freedom within limits); hands-on learning (*see* hands-on learning/experience);

independence (*see* independence); mixed-age grouping 9; observation 9, 22–33, 159; planes of development (*see* planes of development); practical application of 159; prepared environment (*see* prepared environment); respect 9, 19, 107–115; role of adult (*see* adult); sensitive periods 8–9, 44–50

motor skills development 141–142

movement 140; and adult 143–144; benefits of 142; boxes and bottles activity 145–147, *147*; and child 141–142; freedom of 78, 81, 142–144, 151; motor and cognitive development 141–142; and prepared environment 144; purposeful 140, 142–144, 151; refinement of 46; sandpaper letters activities 144, 148, *148–149*; sensitive periods for 46, 117; and sports 150; and wellbeing 150–151

numerals 135–137, *136*

observation 9, *32–33*, 40, 159; and adult 22, 24–25, *33*; benefits 23; calm environment 27; case study 81–82; challenges 27; and child 22–24; in classroom 160; example 28–29; patience in 27; and prepared environment 25–26; record 27; reflecting on 30; sensitive periods 45; skills 25; types of 26; utilising your 29–30; visitor 30

order 17, 53, 57, 59; sensitive periods for 48, 117

outdoor play 70–72, *72–74*, 74

outdoor prepared environment 59–60, *60–61*

peace education 153, 156–157

plane of absorbent mind (0–6 years) 42–43, 156–157; manifestations 37; needs 36; successful education during 37; unconscious *vs.* conscious absorbent mind 37; *see also* absorbent mind

plane of sensorial learner *see* plane of absorbent mind (0–6 years)

planes of development 8, 35–36; commonalities of 36; first (*see* plane of absorbent mind (0–6 years)); periods of growth, children 36–37

play 63; adult-child relationship 66–67; in early childhood development 64–66; with learning 63–66; outdoor 70–72, *72–74*, 74; and prepared environment 68–70, *69–70*; psychologists view 65; quality experiences 67; skills developed through 66; work and 67–68, *69–70*, 70–72, *72–74*, 74

practical life activities 58; aim of 89; basic skills 101; benefits 94–95; boxes and bottles activities 145–147, *147*; examples of 89, *89–92*, 92–94, *94*; independence in setting table 104–106, *105*; mathematics 132; repetition of movement 144; writing 118–119, 126–128

praise and respect 110–111

prepared environment 8, 159; absorbent mind and 41; and adult 52, 57–58; and child 56–57; child, adult and 16–19, *21*; components of 52; examples of *54–56*; features of 17–18, 54; freedom within limits and 80–81; hands-on learning and 88–89; independence and 101–102; language in 119–123, *120–123*; mathematics and 132–133; movement and 144; objectives of 53; observation and 25–26; outdoor 59–60, *60–61*; physical aspects of 58–59; play and 68–70, *69–70*; principles of 50, 53–54, 62; psychological aspects of 57; respect and 109–110; sensitive periods and 49–50; social and emotional development 155–156

psychic phases/planes 36

psychology of child 38

purposeful movement 140, 142–144, 151; *see also* movement

reading: instilling a love of 127–128; writing and 118–119, 126–127

reality, prepared environment 17, 53

record observations 27; *see also* observation

refinement of senses 47–48, 117–118

respect 9, 19, 107–108, 154; and adult 109; case study 112–113; child's work 110; effective/purposeful praise 110; encouragement and praise 111; grace and courtesy lessons 111–114, *114*;

individuality of child 108–109, 112–113; and prepared environment 109–110; principles of 112–113
responsibility: absorbent mind 40–41; freedom and 76, 78
right to play 63, 74; *see also* play

sandpaper letters activities 144, 148, *148–149*
scientific observation 6, 22, 48; *see also* observation
Seguin, E. 5, 123
self-confidence 97, 98
self-esteem 97
self-observation 26–27
sense of community 153, 155, 157
sensitive periods 8–9, 35, 44; and adult 48–49; benefit of awareness 46; and child 45–46, 50; intense focus 45; for language 46–47, 117, 118; for movement 46, 117; observation 45, 48–49; for order 48, 117; and prepared environment 49–50; refinement of movement 46; refinement of senses 47–48, 117–118
sensorial activities 58, 59
social and emotional development 152–157
social embryo 37

social environment, prepared environment 18, 53
social skills 153
sound games 125–126
spindle boxes activity 133–134, *134*
spiritual embryo 38
sports, movement and 150

tactile sense development 84–85
tangible environment, language and 119
the guide *see* adult
three-period lesson, language 123–125

unconscious absorbent mind 35, 37; features 39; *see also* absorbent mind
uninterrupted work periods 103; adult role in 103–104; setting to support independence 103–104
United Nations Conventions on the Rights of the Child (UNCRC) 63, 74

visitor observation 30, *31*

wellbeing: independence and 142–143; movement and 150–151
work and play 67–68, *69–70*, 70–72, *72–74*, 74
writing: physical abilities for 118, 126; and reading 118–119, 126–128

For Product Safety Concerns and Information please contact our EU representative GPSR@taylorandfrancis.com
Taylor & Francis Verlag GmbH, Kaufingerstraße 24, 80331 München, Germany

www.ingramcontent.com/pod-product-compliance
Lightning Source LLC
Chambersburg PA
CBHW072232240426
43670CB00040B/2521